SOCIOLOGICAL
SNAPSHOTS

Adventures in Social Research: Data Analysis Using SPSS for Windows by Earl Babbie and Fred Halley

Race, Ethnicity, Gender, and Class: The Sociology of Group Conflict and Change by Joseph F. Healey

The Production of Reality: Essays and Readings in Social Psychology by Peter Kollock and Jodi O'Brien

Diversity in America by Vincent N. Parrillo

The McDonaldization of Society, Rev. Ed., by George Ritzer

Expressing America: A Critique of the Global Credit Card Society by George Ritzer

Shifts in the Social Contract: Understanding Change in American Society by Beth Rubin

Sociology: Exploring the Architecture of Everyday Life by David M. Newman (text and reader)

The Pine Forge Press Series in Research Methods and Statistics
Edited by Richard T. Campbell and Kathleen S. Crittenden

Investigating the Social World: The Process and Practice of Research by Russell K. Schutt

A Guide to Field Research by Carol A. Bailey

Designing Surveys: A Guide to Decisions and Procedures by Ron Czaja and Johnny Blair

How Sampling Works by Caroline Persell and Richard Maisel

Sociology for a New Century
A Pine Forge Press Series edited by Charles Ragin, Wendy Griswold, and Larry Griffin

- **How Societies Change** by Daniel Chirot
- **Cultures and Societies in a Changing World** by Wendy Griswold
- **Crime and Disrepute** by John Hagan
- **Gods in the Global Village** by Lester R. Kurtz
- **Constructing Social Research** by Charles C. Ragin
- **Women and Men at Work** by Barbara Reskin and Irene Padavic

SOCIOLOGICAL SNAPSHOTS

Seeing Social Structure and Change in Everyday Life

JACK LEVIN

Northeastern University

PINE FORGE PRESS
Thousand Oaks, California ▪ *London* ▪ *New Delhi*

For information address:

Pine Forge Press
A Sage Publications Company
2455 Teller Road
Thousand Oaks, California 91320

SAGE Publications Ltd.
6 Bonhill Street
London EC2A 4PU
United Kingdom

SAGE Publications India Pvt. Ltd.
M-32 Market
Greater Kailash I
New Delhi 110 048 India

Production Manager: Rebecca Holland
Production Editor: Gillian Dickens
Designer Text and Cover: Lisa S. Mirski
Desktop Typesetter: Christina Hill

Photo credits: Page 21 © Danuta Otfinowski 1981, Jeroboam, Inc.; page 49
© Olof Källström 1984, Jeroboam, Inc.; page 75 © Karen R. Preuss 1978,
Jeroboam, Inc.; page 93 © James Motlow 1978, Jerobaum, Inc.; page 111 ©
Frank Siteman 1989, Jeroboam, Inc.; page 135 © Frank Siteman 1985,
Jeroboam, Inc.; page 155 © Kent Reno 1981, Jeroboam, Inc.

Printed in the United States of America

1 2 3 4 5 6 7 8 9 10 — 99 98 97 96

Library of Congress Cataloging-in-Publication Data

Levin, Jack, 1941–
    Sociological snapshots 2 : seeing social structure and change in
everyday life / Jack Levin. — [2nd ed.]
        p.   cm.
    Includes bibliographical references and index.
    ISBN 0-8039-9075-8
    1. Sociology. 2. Social change. 3. Social structure—United
States. 4. United States—Social conditions—1980–   I. Title.
HM51.L3587 1995
301—dc20   95-8239

Contents

About the Author

Jack Levin is Professor of Sociology and Criminology at Northeastern University. He has authored and coauthored a number of books, including *Elementary Statistics in Social Research*, *The Functions of Discrimination and Prejudice*, *Gossip: The Inside Scoop*, *Hate Crimes: The Rising Tide of Bigotry and Bloodshed*, and *Overkill: Mass Murder and Serial Killing Exposed*. His work has appeared in professional journals, including *Youth & Society*, *Criminology*, *The Gerontologist*, and *Sex Roles*, as well as in the *New York Times*, the *Boston Globe*, the *Detroit Free Press*, and the *Chicago Tribune*. He has lectured on campuses across the country.

A dedicated educator and social advocate, Jack Levin received Northeastern University's Excellence in Teaching Award and was recently honored by the Council for Advancement and Support of Education as its Professor of the Year in Massachusetts.

■ ABOUT THE PUBLISHER

Pine Forge Press is a new educational publisher, dedicated to publishing innovative books and software throughout the social sciences. On this and any other of our publications, we welcome your comments and suggestions. Please call or write us at

PINE FORGE PRESS
A Sage Publications Company
2455 Teller Road
Thousand Oaks, CA 91320
(805) 499-4224
E-mail: sales@pfp.sagepub.com

Preface

Sociology is a vitally exciting field. You may know that and I may know that. The trick is getting our students to realize it. Usually, instructors who teach introductory sociology hope that they will develop in their students some enthusiasm for the contributions of the field—but the question is always *how.*

I wrote this book with at least two specific outcomes in mind, both of which relate to the general goal of getting the students to understand and appreciate the sociological perspective:

1. to serve as a springboard to more abstract thinking about society, and

2. to encourage student interest in learning more about the field of sociology.

It is an important function of sociology to help broaden the educational experience of all college students, but especially those in fields of study that may be narrow in scope and purpose. One measure of the effectiveness of an introductory sociology course is the extent to which students come to view their world with a sociological eye.

When students truly "see" the sociology in things, they are also being helped to develop their abstract thinking skills—the very skills that are of vital importance in any job or career. Unfortunately, students too often get little help from their introductory courses in enhancing their ability to think at an abstract level. Instead, they are asked to read and memorize long lists of terms that seem more to obfuscate and complicate than to clarify reality.

The snapshots in this book are casual and informal, but they are designed to ease students into the formal world of sociological analysis. Each essay relates some abstract sociological concepts to the concrete problems confronting ordinary people. Social structure and social change are introduced as major variables but almost always in the context of everyday life.

At the same time, the snapshots are grounded in sociological data and theorizing. The introductory essays that lead each section are intended to emphasize the importance of the formal sociological literature. Indeed, the entire book serves as a springboard from the informal, concrete world of the student to the more formal, abstract world of sociological theory and method.

Students also need active ways for developing their ability to see and articulate abstractions and for analyzing data about social reality. The physical and biological sciences usually include a "lab" component in their courses in which students are given an opportunity for hands on experience. Sociologists should attempt, wherever possible, to do the same.

For this reason, each section of the book contains ideas for student writing and research assignments. There is nothing fancy or complicated about the proposed tasks. They are designed to get introductory students to begin to write from a sociological perspective or to collect data about their everyday lives. We can only hope that they will decide to go on to bigger and better sociological things.

To the extent that the first outcome is realized, students will, I hope, also achieve the second: They will be eager to learn more about the sociological perspective. Some will take more sociology courses or even major in the discipline.

Unlike the situation in many other fields, sociology simply cannot depend on students' prior familiarity with the study of behavior to provide a background of information or enhance their interest. In high school, very few had the opportunity to select a sociology course. Some may have a vague idea that sociologists study human behavior or that sociology is somehow related to social work, but that's about it.

Partly as a result of their lack of familiarity, only a small number of students declare a sociology major when entering college: More typically, students who enroll in introductory sociology courses represent a range of disciplines and interests. It is, therefore, a major function of the introductory sociology course—for many undergraduates, perhaps their only point of formal contact—to convince students to take upper-level courses in the field. This places a special burden on instructors to provide a positive learning climate—one in which student interest is encouraged.

Writing the second edition of *Sociological Snapshots* has given me a chance to make improvements and correct mistakes. Most of the snapshots found in the first edition have been retained, although a few have been placed in a different section, modified, or updated. I have added two new sections—The Group Experience and Institutions—in response to the suggestions of instructors and reviewers. The introductory section has been completely overhauled. Moreover, there are nine new snapshots in this edition, seven of which were written specifically for the book.

A number of people were important in making *Sociological Snapshots 2* a reality. At *Bostonia*, I am grateful to Laura Freid who gave me the opportunity to write a regular column on behavior for a first-rate magazine, to Keith Botsford who permitted me to carry on the tradition, and to Lori Calabro and Janice Friedman under whose skillful editorship the quality of my writing always improved. I also thank David Gibson at *Northeastern University Magazine* for helping me to write the essay concerning the sociology of soap operas. Rachelle Cohen encouraged me to do "Race, IQ, and Hysterectomies" for the *Boston Herald*, and Marjorie Pritchard encouraged me to write "Who's Minding the Kids?" for the *Boston Globe*.

I also depended a great deal on the insightful comments and suggestions of the following reviewers:

Paul Baker, *Illinois State University*
Agnes Riedmann, *Creighton University*
Anne Hastings, *University of North Carolina at Chapel Hill*
Robert Emerick, *San Diego State University*
Judith Richlin-Klonsy, *University of California, Los Angeles*
William R. Aho, *Rhode Island College*
Russ Crescimanno, *Piedmont Community College*
Diane Carmody, *Western Washington University*
Judith Lawler Caron, *Albertus Magnus College*
Mary Rogers, *University of West Florida*
Michael L. Sanow, *Towson State University*
Rich Eckstein, *Villanova University*
Shirley Varmette, *Southern Connecticut State*

My colleague Arnie Arluke deserves a special note of praise for suggesting the title of this book. Jamie Fox and Bill Levin were generous with both their encouragement and their ideas.

Steve Rutter of Pine Forge Press made all the difference. If he made me slave over a "hot" PC, then it was worth every minute. No editor could have done more.

My wife, Flea, and my children, Michael, Bonnie, and Andrea have been more than patient, tolerating all of my idiosyncrasies.

As in the earlier edition, I dedicate this book to the thousands of students I have had the pleasure of teaching. They have taught me a great deal about sociology and about life.

JACK LEVIN
BOSTON, MASSACHUSETTS

THE SOCIOLOGICAL EYE

Among my several hobbies, photography is my favorite. I've never tried to take formal or posed pictures. Instead, the heart of my interest—what I have always found most satisfying—is the art of taking "snapshots"—informal, often candid, photos of everyday life. I particularly enjoy capturing on film the problems experienced by ordinary people as well as the spontaneous, unguarded moments in the lives of loved ones.

The essays in this book are snapshots, too, but they are sociological snapshots. Each one is a "3 × 5 glossy" of a social situation encountered by the people we meet every day—the circumstances of ordinary people caught up in ordinary (and, occasionally, not so ordinary) social events. You will find essays about family and class reunions, television soap operas, behavior in elevators, children who have unpopular names, the people who do dirty work in occupations, spectators at football games, bystander apathy, people who act in deviant ways while driving in automobiles, heartburn, fads through the generations, popular rumors about shopping malls, contemporary images of fat people, and so on. At the extreme end, you will also discover a few essays concerning topics such as the death penalty, mass killers, and hate crimes (sadly, in today's society, even ordinary people have to be aware of such extraordinary topics).

The essays in this book are snapshots in another sense as well; most take a casual, informal approach with respect to the presentation of statistical evidence. Many appeared originally in *Bostonia* (a magazine of "culture and ideas"). Others were opinion pieces that I earlier published in newspapers. Some were written specifically for this book. But all of them were designed to bridge the gap existing between the "two cultures" of academic sociology and everyday life. As a result, in every snapshot, you will find a mix of both social science and journalism. There are very few references, quantitative data, and formal evidence, the kind that you typically expect to find in an introductory sociology textbook. Sometimes, the essays in the book present only anecdotal confirmation—illustrations and examples rather than hard, statistical fact. Some are speculative pieces about changes in society or about the future. Others seek to throw a new perspective on aspects of society that may have seemed obvious to you before. None is meant to replace the technical journal articles written for professional sociologists. All are meant to motivate students, to help them see the contribution of the sociological approach, and to ease them as gently as possible into the more formal world of sociological analysis.

After teaching classes in sociology for a number of years, I have noticed that many students are troubled by what they regard as the abstractness of sociological insight. They often complain about not being able to see how social structure touches their everyday lives or how culture contributes to ordinary events. No longer are they asked to examine the structure of individuals but of entire groups, organizations, institutions, communities, or societies.

What I believe is missing, from a pedagogical viewpoint, are the snapshots of culture and social structure that bridge the gap existing in many students' minds between what may appear to be vast sociological abstractions, on the one hand, and everyday experiences, on the other. Hence, the central purpose of this book: to relate abstract sociological concepts to the concrete problems confronting ordinary individuals in our society.

But please don't be fooled into believing that these snapshots represent the personal opinions of the author alone. On the contrary, all of them are based on either sociological thinking, sociological data, or both. The essays that introduce each section of the book and the annotated suggested readings at the end ("Focus: Suggestions for Further Reading") are meant to emphasize the importance of the sociological literature. Indeed, they direct the student to it. You will find that the suggested readings include not only the more formal sources on which the snapshots were based but also important general works from the sociological literature. I have tried to describe them in enough detail so that interested students will understand *why* they might be worth reading. Once again, no snapshot is meant to replace the technical journal articles—the formal portraits—written for professional sociologists, but all are grounded in them.

Nor was this book written to replace your standard introductory text. Instead, *Sociological Snapshots* was intended to serve as a springboard into the formal course material, whether presented in a single text or as a series of monographs. To move back and forth between levels of abstraction, each section of the book has been organized in a consistent format. First, there is an introductory essay in which the basic sociological concepts are defined, discussed, illustrated, and then linked with the snapshots for that particular section. Second, there are the snapshots themselves. Next, there are suggestions for further reading, extensively annotated (see the Bibliography for publication information for each reading). Finally, there are ideas for student writing and research assignments in "Developing Ideas." By the way, most of these assignments require the students to apply a sociological eye to their everyday lives or to *begin*, in a preliminary way, to collect data using a sociological method.

There is one final sense in which the essays in this book are snapshots. They often reflect, frequently in an explicit way, the ideas that the "photographer" considers to be valuable or problematic. In taking pictures of the world around me, I often take photos of my family and friends, and occasionally of the unusual circumstances of daily life, but always with a point of view implicit in my choice of subject. In other words, my snapshots are, in part, a reflection of my values—the things that I appreciate or cherish. They are often addressed to preserving and understanding the images of the people I love, the problems in everyday life that bother me, or the things I believe need changing.

Like all "scientists," sociologists have values. They are human beings too, having grown up in a particular social setting and having been exposed selectively to certain kinds of ideas.

Max Weber, a turn-of-the-century German sociologist who contributed a great deal to our understanding of religion, inequality, and social change, strongly believed that sociology could be *value-free*. He fully recognized that the subjects sociologists chose to study were frequently influenced by their personal values. For example, it would not be surprising that a sociologist who grew up in extreme poverty might decide to study inequality; a rape victim might conduct research into the causes of sexual violence; an African American sociologist might specialize in race relations; and so on.

But when Weber talked about value-free sociology, he really wasn't talking about the selection of a subject about which to conduct research. Instead, he meant that sociologists must not permit their values, their biases, or their personal opinions to interfere with their analysis of that subject. They must, instead, attempt to be objective in collecting and analyzing information; they must seek out and consider *all* of the evidence, even evidence that might contradict their personal opinions. Weber would have advised that we must "let the chips fall where they may." I hope my personal biases have determined only the subjects of my snapshots, not the conclusions that I reach about them.

Now that you understand the "snapshot" part of the title of this book, *Sociological Snapshots 2*, I ask that you stop a moment longer and consider the "sociological" part as well. As you probably already surmise—even if you have never taken a course in it—psychology deals with the behavior and personality of *individual* human beings. Psychologists might study a person's attitudes, hostility, attractiveness, moods, helpfulness, learning styles, prejudices, and so on. In contrast, sociologists focus not on any one individual but on what happens *between* two or more individuals when they interact. Sociologists might study the relationship between husband and wife, interaction in a small task group at work, the peer groups in a high school, family relations, prison culture, relations between managers and workers, and so on.

To explain the unique and important contribution of sociology, allow me to reveal a little bit about my everyday routine. Every time I drive from my suburban home to my office in the city, I think about how painfully predictable and orderly my daily commuting routine has become. I live some 25 miles from downtown; so I have plenty of time, while sitting in bumper-to-bumper traffic, to think. In my darker, more impatient moments, I play "what if" games: "What if I had sold my house and moved into the city?" "What if I were teaching in a college located in a remote, rural area?" "What if I had taken the train into work?" "What if I could change my schedule to avoid the rush hour commute?" *Would I still be stuck in traffic? Probably not.*

As a sociologist, the interesting thing about my predicament is the fact that it is shared by so many other people. This, of course, explains why traffic jams happen on a daily basis. Tens of thousands of residents have similar work schedules, live in the suburbs, and drive their cars to work in the city. They get up at about the same time every morning, take a shower, brush their teeth, and have a cup of coffee. Then, they take to the roads—most of them at the same time that I do!

Sociologists seek to understand the predictable and *patterned* aspects of what happens between people when they get together; sociologists even have a term for it: *social structure*. And in the case of sitting in maddening bumper-to-bumper traffic every day, social structure has become my biggest headache.

The negative consequences of social structure can be seen in other ways as well. In "Better Late Than Never," we see that college students are usually expected to "bloom" on time. That is, they are supposed to excel academically from an early age and to enter college by the age of 18 or 19. Indeed, if they vary from the expected pattern, students are given a name. They are called "late bloomers."

Of course, whether or not a student is ultimately successful in the classroom (and in a career) is partially a matter of individual effort, talent, and luck. But there is definitely an important sociological side to being successful as well. *You probably won't excel academically if you are denied the opportunity to do so.*

Traditionally, men were much more likely than women, no matter how qualified in terms of grades and test scores, to be given any opportunity for higher education. Similarly, it was far more probable for individuals who are born into wealthy circumstances to attend college than for their economically less fortunate counterparts.

Opportunity also varies by society. In most societies, blooming on time is strictly enforced, no matter how much potential an individual might have. You either go to college at the age of 18 or not at all; you either get As and Bs by the time you're 12 years old or you receive a trade school education, at best. In American society, we still prefer blooming on schedule—the majority of college students fit the mold, but we also allow some flexibility as to timing. In fact, 25% of all college students are now over 30; and close to 20% of college freshmen had Cs and Ds in high school.

Of course, social structure also has its desirable aspects. Because social life is somewhat predictable, we are able to count on instructors meeting their classes, count on doctors making their appointments, count on final exams to begin and end pretty much on time, and so on. Because of the strict scheduling of time in an educational context, school administrators definitely benefit, because they can predict with some degree of certainty precisely how many textbooks, classrooms, and teachers they will need for an upcoming academic year. In fact, it would not be too much of an exaggeration to suggest that life without some degree of social order—social structure—would be utterly chaotic and therefore impossible over the long run. Perhaps the rush-hour commute is unpleasant, but at least we can be fairly sure that classes will be held when scheduled and that shops, stores, and restaurants will be open when they are expected to be.

In "Heartburn and Modern Times," I suggest that even basic biological processes (the regurgitation of stomach acid back into the esophagus causing the burning sensation we call *heartburn*) may be influenced by a weakening of social structure. French sociologist Emile Durkheim, who lived at the turn of the century, used the term *anomie* to describe a social situation in which the traditional rules of everyday life have broken down and individuals become confused as to how to behave. Because of a sudden and dramatic change in lifestyle, their old patterns of social interaction are disturbed and new patterns have not yet been established. Individuals caught in an anomic condition are therefore at a loss to know how they are expected to behave. Social life is, for them, no longer patterned, shared, or predictable.

A state of anomie can be brought on by any of several different circumstances—for example, war, a physical disaster, a dramatic drop in income, or the loss of family and friends. Communities that attract large numbers of transients, drifters, and migrants often experience anomic conditions. For example, many who move great distances from home for the sake of a job have left behind all sources of guidance and support—their friends, extended kin, church, and fraternal organizations. After arriving in Los Angeles or Miami or Houston, they may have no place to turn for counsel or advice.

In his classic work, Durkheim discovered that anomie actually provoked some individuals to commit suicide. More precisely, he found that the rate of suicide in an area increases during periods of rapid social or economic change and also among those who are recently divorced or widowed. If anomie affects the rate of suicide, it should be less than shocking to discover that anomie produces high rates of antacid use as well. Indeed, anomic circumstances seem to be associated with all forms of pathology, including crime, suicide, and even heartburn. Notice, by the way, that I address the *rate* of pathology, including antacid use, rather than any individual who experiences heartburn. I am not suggesting that the newcomers in any metropolitan area necessarily suffer with heartburn (though this is possible), only that their presence in large numbers will increase the likelihood that the heartburn rate is generally high. Maybe it's the transients and drifters who have heartburn; or perhaps they give it to more stable members of the population. As a sociologist, I am characterizing the metropolitan area as a whole, even if I never look at an individual case. In sum: The state of some characteristic of the area (its degree of migration) may have some influence on its rate of acid indigestion, not to mention its rate of suicide, homicide, and divorce. ∎

Better Late Than Never
Individual Success Doesn't Always Follow a Strict Schedule

Dr. William Levin is a professor of sociology at Bridgewater State College, an award-winning teacher, and the prolific author of a number of respected books in his field. He also flunked the eighth grade.

I met Bill Levin almost 20 years ago as his master's thesis adviser in what was then the School of Public Communication at Boston University. We hit it off almost immediately. Not only did we share the same last name (though not the same parents), but we also discovered we were both educational late bloomers—mediocre high school students who later developed into serious-minded, dedicated college students (I can't say that I flunked the eighth grade, but I can still "brag" about being on academic probation during my first year as an undergraduate at American International College).

Bill Levin's escape from educational mediocrity is far from unique. In fact, there are thousands of educational late bloomers who go on to become brilliant college or graduate students. Thousands more interrupt their collegiate pursuits, only to return years later. In fact, we live in a society in which second chances are fast becoming a way of life, especially in the educational field.

We tolerate late blooming, but do we know why? Trying to answer just that question, Bill and I recently talked with a number of college students. And in interviews with both late and early bloomers, we were able to identify four important factors: capacity, opportunity, some triggering event, and a period of readiness to accept change in which social support is present.

Intellectual capacity is a prerequisite for almost any success, whenever it occurs in the life cycle. But for late bloomers, capacity has an important emotional component. Those who lack intellectual capacity more than make up for it with commitment and involvement. Many of the late bloomers we interviewed were, as high school students, almost fanatically devoted to a cause, a hobby, a job, a sport, or an idea. For example, while in high school, one late bloomer became committed to physical exercise. Hard-pressed to find the time to study, he still managed to jog, run, lift weights, bike, and swim on a regular basis. Another student was heavily into illicit drugs. He spent hours in the library, but not doing his homework. Instead, he read and researched articles related to his addiction. Then there was the mechanical engineering major who now has a 3.6 grade point average but had only a 2.5 average in high school. He, however, was a member of his school's debating team and chorus in addition to working more than 20 hours a week.

In a sense, the presence of emotional commitment in high school may indicate later academic potential. The question is how do we transfer that commitment from an extracurricular activity, athletics, or a cause to the college classroom?

Part of the answer involves the second factor in late blooming: the presence of opportunity. Almost everywhere outside the United States, the timing of academic success is inflexible. Students must achieve high grades and achievement test scores early in their academic careers; they must also enter college by a specified age. In England, India, and Japan, for example, students who have not excelled by the time they reach high school are effectively disqualified as college material. What is more, students are expected to enroll in college by their late teens and are not given opportunities to do so later in life, regardless of their potential. Even after the educational reforms of the post-World War II era, highly structured lines of study separating high school attendance from access to college remain the modal pattern around the rest of the world.

In sharp contrast, the American educational system gives students a second, third, even a fourth chance for a college education. If they or their parents are able to pay the bills, even students who have low grades in high school are granted an opportunity to enroll in higher education. One third of all colleges have open admission policies. Moreover, hundreds of thousands of students who begin at community and junior colleges later transfer into 4-year institutions. The increasing number of women who return to college after raising children provides a significant new pool of potential late bloomers. Similarly, the increasing acceptance of midlife career changes has created an entirely new category of late, late bloomers who continue their education after spending decades in the workforce.

But capacity and opportunity are not always enough for late blooming to occur. Bill Levin, for example, had the opportunity to attend college because his parents saved the money to send him. And like millions of other middle-class students, he went to college primarily because that's what was expected of him. But for Levin and others like him, the commitment to education only materialized because of a triggering event—a reward, a punishment, or both that provided a rationale for making a profound change in their lifestyle.

For some of the late bloomers we studied, that triggering event was a work experience during college. Some suggested that a job showed them, perhaps for the first time, the strong connection between grades and the kind of work they were likely to do after they graduated. Even an unpleasant job during college was motivating; it forced them to deal with the likelihood that unless things changed drastically, this was the kind of boring, monotonous work they might expect to be doing for the rest of their lives.

Other late bloomers pointed to more positive events as triggering their commitment to academics. Some, such as Bill Levin, gave credit to a great teacher who had inspired them to study or to a course that was new and exciting to them. Others were a few years older than their classmates, having dropped out to work for a year or two, transferred from another college, or spent a few years in the military. Peers also made a difference. For example, one late-blooming college senior reported that it was a bright, achievement-oriented girlfriend who motivated him by threatening to end their relationship if he didn't "buckle down."

If the series of triggering events is effective, a student enters a period of readiness to change when social support and encouragement become extremely important. During this stage, the academic community gradually becomes an important reference point, a source of norms and values as well as a source of guidance. The student frequently changes his or her major based on personal interest rather than practicality or parental guidance. For the first time, grades are used as markers of personal worth and school takes on primary importance.

The individual is ready to bloom. He talks informally with instructors during their office hours and after classes; she discusses a lecture with her friends. He spends more time in the library; she writes for the campus newspaper and runs for student government. In this stage, instructors, advisers, and friends can make a huge difference. The student is ready to bloom, but he or she still looks for and needs the help of others on campus.

At the time I first met Bill Levin, he had recently discovered the social sciences. Within a year, he had become totally immersed in graduate student culture. Like so many of his early-blooming classmates, he read, talked, and slept sociology; it became the focal point of his life.

It is legitimate to ask whether it is worth focusing so much attention on late bloomers. After all, aren't they less successful than their counterparts who achieve "on time"? Actually, one of the few studies to compare late and early bloomers concludes just the opposite. Scientists whose educational achievements came relatively late were more productive than those scientists who achieved early. Educational burnout may be less severe for late bloomers, not only because they begin later to achieve in earnest but also because they are more likely to achieve for their own sake rather than for the sake of a parent. The success of a late bloomer may be particularly sweet. You've heard the expression, "Better late than never." Have you ever considered the possibility, "Better late than early," at least where education is concerned?

Given our present state of knowledge, we are not able to predict who will and will not turn out to be a late bloomer. Until our theories and methods permit such accurate predictions, we must treat every student as a potential late bloomer. This means that we must never give up on anyone. Bill Levin is living proof and he has plenty of company. ∎

Heartburn and Modern Times
Don't Blame the Tex-Mex

According to a Gallup survey conducted several years ago, the ailment known as heartburn is a chronic source of pain and suffering for almost 62 million American adults. Fifty-four percent of them pin the blame on spicy foods; others single out overeating, indigestion, gas, or poor diet. Many regularly take an antacid in pill or liquid form.

For the sufferer, heartburn clearly has a biological basis. It frequently occurs after a meal when acid backs up from the stomach into the esophagus, causing a burning sensation in the chest or throat. From a sociological point of view, however, there may be a good deal more to heartburn than just the discomfort of spicy foods and excessive acidity. Like many other physical ailments, the symptoms of heartburn may be influenced by the stresses and strains frequently associated with residential mobility undertaken to enhance a career or supposedly improve the quality of life.

I ranked 197 metropolitan areas of the United States on the "National Rolaids Heartburn Index," a measure based on an area's per-capita sales of all brands of over-the-counter antacids, and then compared these metropolitan areas on a grid of important social, economic, and demographic characteristics. Most striking, I found important regional differences in heartburn rates. For example, despite their reputation for having a laid-back pace of life, most major cities located in the far West—San Francisco, Sacramento, Fresno, Seattle, Los Angeles, and Phoenix—had particularly high rates of antacid use. Indeed, 40% of all high-heartburn metropolitan areas were located in western states. Also having particularly high rates were southern cities such as Charlotte, North Carolina; Richmond, Virginia; and New Orleans, Louisiana.

By contrast, midwestern cities had extremely low rates of heartburn. Green Bay, Wisconsin; Sioux City, Iowa; Columbia, Missouri; and Fort Smith, Arkansas, placed close to the bottom. In fact, almost half of the 40 metropolitan areas with the lowest rates of heartburn were located in midwestern states. But the lowest of them all was located in El Paso, Texas, which, with its penchant for spicy Tex-Mex cuisine, turned out to have the lowest level of heartburn of any city in the United States.

Data on northeastern cities were also surprising. Overall, those cities seldom exhibited either high or low heartburn levels. Only 11% of both the highest heartburn metropolitan areas and the lowest heartburn areas were located in the Northeast. New York City, for example, registered only a moderate rate of heartburn, though it is well-known for its fast-paced, hectic way of life.

How can these variations in rates of antacid use by metropolitan area be explained? Differences in diet and physical environment might contribute to the overall level of heartburn. Over-the-counter antacid use may not be an accurate measure of heartburn (a few people without heartburn take these antacids and many with heartburn do not).

Despite such methodological problems, a major contributing factor to the rate of heartburn in an area can be found in what might be called "gold rush fever." All of the cities with a high incidence of heartburn have recently experienced tremendous population growth as a result of migration from other cities and regions of the country. For the sake of a job or a better way of life, former midwesterners and easterners have "gone west." They have packed their bags, left behind family and friends, and traveled thousands of miles to cities on the West Coast. This may explain why most of the most attractive and appealing metropolitan areas also have the highest rates of heartburn. They attract individuals who are dissatisfied with their present lives and are willing to move to enhance it.

Cities with stable populations are more likely to have a low incidence of heartburn. These cities appeal less to individuals who want to increase their economic opportunities. In such cities, construction comes to a standstill as the demand for real estate remains constant. Of the top 15 housing markets, not one is located in a low-heartburn metropolitan area, but 5 are in the high-heartburn group. The city of El Paso never experienced the oil-based, boom-and-bust cycle of heartburn-plagued Texas cities such as Dallas or Houston.

Wherever there are large numbers of transient, rootless people, there is also likely to be anxiety, stress, frustration . . . and high levels of heartburn. Sociologists call this state of affairs *anomie*, a social condition that prevails where newcomers to an area are confused as to the rules of living. When things are anomic, there is widespread disorganization and isolation, a breakdown in order.

One indicator of anomie is the presence of social pathology. Thus, high-heartburn areas were more likely than their low-heartburn counterparts to also have high rates of violent crime, divorce, and alcohol consumption. Heartburn may be another, albeit more subtle, indicator that something is wrong.

Other researchers have noticed that the pathology varies by specific metropolitan areas. Social psychologist Robert Levine of California State University recently compared cities in terms of their level of psychological stress. He found that 6 of his 10 cities with highest stress were located in the far West. He determined that stress was especially high in those metropolitan areas that contained large numbers of migrants, residents who were born out of state. Not coincidentally, the western states had the greatest percentage of migrants—gold rush fever strikes again!

Census Bureau data suggest that the population flow to the far West may be on the verge of reversing itself. In the future, easterners and midwesterners may cease exporting their heartburn to other areas of the country. Who knows? New York, Philadelphia, or Boston might even become the next heartburn capital of the United States. ∎

■ **FOCUS** *Suggestions for Further Reading*

Concerning "Better Late Than Never," Bill Levin and I published our ideas about late blooming in an article titled "Sociology of Educational Late-Blooming," in *Sociological Forum* (1991). More recently, I wrote more about the triggering incidents for late blooming in "Misery as a Turning Point for Academic Success," in *Journal of Research in Education* (1993).

Eviatar Zurubavel's book, *Hidden Rhythms: Schedules and Calendars in Social Life* (1981), offers insights into a much neglected topic, the sociology of time. For a social-historical analysis of the rise of age consciousness in American society, read Howard Chudacoff's *How Old Are You?* (1989). In this fascinating work, he reminds us that there was a time when people didn't know their precise ages and when birthdays were left uncelebrated. Prior to the 20th century, people rarely sent birthday cards to one another or had birthday parties.

The data reported in "Heartburn and Modern Times" concerning rates of antacid use by metropolitan area were originally collected by pollster A. C. Nielson. I was hired by Warner Lambert to analyze these data and then report my results to them.

The link between heartburn and anomie is a new variation on an old theme. Anomic circumstances have long been associated with high rates of pathology. In his classic study *Suicide: A Study in Sociology* (1951), Émile Durkheim introduces a sociological theory to explain differences in the rate of suicide by time and place. One of his major types is called "anomic suicide" because it results from a sharp break, a profound disruption in the social bond.

The powerful attraction of social structure is poignantly illustrated in Debra Renee Kaufman's excellent account of *Rachel's Daughters* (1991). Her subjects were women who returned to religious orthodoxy out of a sense that structure was missing from their lives. By contrast, the extraordinary women in Mary Catherine Bateson's *Composing a Life* (1990) chose a different course in response to ambiguities in the female role. Making the best of the severe discontinuities in their lives, they improvised opportunities for creativity and innovation, but not without experiencing pain.

■ DEVELOPING IDEAS *About Social Structure*

1. Writing topic: In the essay about educational late bloomers, I presented several factors that seem to contribute to succeeding behind schedule, including intellectual capacity, opportunity, a precipitating incident, and social support. Think of someone you know (perhaps a friend or a relative) who possessed the intelligence to bloom educationally but never did. In a short essay, explain how his or her position in the social structure (gender identity, age, socioeconomic status, societal membership) may have helped prevent his or her educational success.

2. Writing topic: In the essay about heartburn, I focused on per-capita antacid use by metropolitan area. How do you think a psychologist who was interested in the causes of heartburn would have conducted this study? Would he or she have examined a number of metropolitan areas? What do you think he or she would have looked for in those individuals who suffered from heartburn? What conclusions might a psychologist have drawn and how might they have differed from those derived by a sociologist?

3. Research topic: One measure of the importance of being on time is just how precisely individuals keep their clocks and watches running. Because the importance of precise time varies from society to society, it is possible that the precision of watches and clocks also varies from place to place. Because it is unreasonable to ask you to travel to another society, instead, compare the clocks and watches in your own home, apartment, or dormitory floor with those in someone else's home, apartment, or dormitory floor. (You might, for example, compare men's and women's floors to determine the influence of gender on the importance of time, or you might compare different kinds of office buildings). In writing, record the error (from actual time) on each clock or watch and then take an average for each place. Also include the number of watches and clocks in a state of disrepair. Now, identify the winner!

4. Writing topic: Instant millionaires—those who win the Megabucks lottery—aren't always as happy as you might believe. Many of them experience tremendous anomie. In a short essay, speculate as to exactly how the lives of instant millionaires might abruptly change . . . for the worse. Also indicate what

you think they might do to minimize the "pain" of suddenly being wealthy.

5. Research topic: Interview someone who has recently experienced a dramatic change in lifestyle—an individual who has moved thousands of miles, has been recently widowed or divorced, or even married. (It would be great, but very difficult, to interview an instant millionaire!) Try to determine whether the abrupt change in that person's way of life has had any negative effects of which he or she is aware. Where does he or she go for help and guidance? Is he or she more anxious about the future? How does that person fill the hours of the day with meaningful activities? If he or she has had little or no trouble adjusting, you might want to determine why. Through friendships, religion, fraternal organizations, or a commitment to work, has that person found a new source of structure in his or her life? ■

PART ONE

Culture

Several of the students in the course I teach on the sociology of violence came from other countries to attend school in Boston. Two were from Asia, one was from Europe, one was from South America, and one was from an island in the Caribbean. About 15 minutes into our first meeting, I realized that their presence in the classroom would make a difference in the way I approached the course. It really didn't take a psychic to figure out that communication would be more difficult. From the first day, there were lots of bewildered looks and blank stares to remind me. Then there were questions.

At first, I considered the problem to be only one of language. In plain English, I believed that my plain English was, to them, not so plain. By the end of our first session together, however, I recognized that the problem was more profound than just misunderstood words and phrases. Indeed, from the types of questions they were asking, I concluded that some of the international students in my class also lacked familiarity with those practices, objects, and ideas that most Americans share on an everyday basis and therefore take for granted as the "American way of life." My foreign students were, in a word, unfamiliar with American *culture*. Consider a concrete example. In our discussion of the manner in which mass killings are reported by the mass media, I introduced James Huberty's 1984 rampage through a McDonald's fast-food restaurant located in a suburb of San Diego. I noted that several newspapers around the country had referred to Huberty's killing spree (he killed 21, mostly Hispanic children) as "Mass McMurder" and "The Big Mac Attack." The American students immediately understood the glib, possibly offensive, aspects of these newspaper headlines, but three of the international students had only questions: "What is a Big Mac?" one asked. Not knowing the logo of this famous hamburger chain, another wanted to know why the paper called Huberty's attack "McMurder." Before continuing our discussion of mass killings, therefore, we spent several minutes talking about fast-food hamburgers.

Now, it is true that degree of familiarity with American culture varies quite a bit among the peoples of the world. And among my international students, I noticed immense variation in this respect. In fact, the young woman from Western Europe was quite familiar with American values and customs, at least much more so than her counterparts from Asia or South America. Though she had been in the United States only a few days before the course began, she had eaten many times in American fast-food restaurants (McDonald's are located throughout Western Europe), had watched American television, and was also acquainted more with the American brand of humor. That's because the values and customs in her own country were so similar to ours. They are likely to be, of course, because we Americans have had enormous contact with Europe and have derived much of our culture from it. The process whereby cultural traits spread from one society to another (e.g., from "the Mother Country" England to the United States) is known as *cultural diffusion*.

Clearly, we can thank (or blame) cultural diffusion for giving us many important ideas and objects that originated in or, at least passed first through, Europe. In "The Immaculate Americans," we discover that it was the British who, during the Industrial Revolution, were plumbing pioneers. By the early part of the 20th century, however, the idea of plumbing for the masses had transversed the Atlantic Ocean, and American society had taken the lead in developing private bathrooms for the majority of its citizens. For the first time in history, the home bathroom was regarded as a middle-class necessity. Also in "The Immaculate Americans," we learn that collective tolerance for odor varies from place to place, from one society to another. In some other parts of the world, Americans are viewed as neurotically concerned with their personal cleanliness. We certainly do use tremendous amounts of deodorant and mouthwash; such products have become part of our culture.

The ideas that we often take for granted or believe to be constants in nature—for example, our ideas about cleanliness—may actually originate in the culture that we learn. But what is the origin of culture? We know that people aren't born with it—although they are born with the *capacity* for culture. Only humans seem to have the full-blown capability; other animals often share a way of life but not one that is learned and passed along to the next generation. For the most part, animals are programmed from birth to act and react in social situations. (For example, birds don't learn to fly by watching other birds do it first; nor do mother birds teach them. They develop the ability for flight by instinct alone.)

The origin of a particular type of cultural content—whether one or another thing is regarded as proper and right—is also a fascinating question. Some sociologists and anthropologists believe that economics may play a major role in determining the particular character of a culture. The important 19th-century theorist Karl Marx argued, in writing about the rise of communism, that the economic system of a society determines almost everything about other social institutions. He believed that religion, family life, and the press were all "handmaidens" to the prevailing economic system; that is, they existed essentially to support and maintain the economic status quo, to make sure that it survived. From a Marxian point of view, therefore, the Protestant belief about work—the religious conviction that hard work is a sign of personal salvation—exists only because capitalism needs a way to dupe or mislead workers; that is, a way of motivating workers to tolerate their terrible working conditions, accept their exploitation by the owners of production, and be achievement oriented in the interest of maximizing corporate profit.

You don't have to accept Marxism to agree that he was right to emphasize the role of the economy in determining the complexion of "mass" culture—popular art and music—in a capitalistic society like ours. Middle-aged rock musicians such as Van Morrison, Paul Simon, Tom Petty, and Billy Joel may not help to preserve capitalism, but their continuing popularity is probably a result of the appeal they have to huge numbers of people who grew up in the 1960s and 1970s and who are willing to spend their hard-earned money in the interest of nostalgia.

In "Baby Boomers: A Generation Without a Gap," we are introduced to a possibly important source of cultural expression. The baby boomers—that generation of people born between 1946 and 1962—continue to have plenty of cultural clout but only so long as they spend their money. How will they be treated if they give up their credit cards? Only time will tell.

As illustrated in "Hate Crimes Against Women," the darker side of mass culture involves a tendency for popular music, comedy, and motion pictures to express anger against vulnerable individuals and groups in our society. Sociologists have long recognized that sexism (like racism) has a cultural basis; just like any other aspect of culture, sexism is therefore expected to be widely shared, enduring, and learned. This is an important, if subtle, point; because it means that we shouldn't necessarily look for sexism in the most pathological, most deviant members of our society. Instead, sexism is conventional; it often originates in the mainstream, rather than at the margins, of a society.

The "culture of hate" belittles and deprecates females, reflecting a more general, perhaps growing, resentment on the part of American men who sense that their masculine advantage has eroded over time. At the extreme, the culture of hate may support and even encourage violent acts against females. According to Justice Department statistics, crimes against women, for a period of two decades, have been on the rise.

On the more positive side of things, culture often takes on human form and substance. The cultural values cherished by Americans are embodied in the heroes we choose to revere on a collective level. During the opening decades of the 20th century, our cultural heroes were what sociologist Leo Lowenthal in 1961 called "idols of production"—industrial tycoons who served as role models for citizens who accepted some version of the American Dream and aspired to be successful and wealthy . . . *just like their heroes.* By midcentury, however, Americans had instead shifted from idols of production to idols of consumption—the entertainers and sports figures who filled our leisure hours with their music, drama, and athletic prowess.

In "The Demise of Bystander Apathy," I speculate that we have recently undergone yet another major shift in our selection of cultural heroes. Coming out of an era of spectatorship and passivity, we now seem to admire "idols of activism," those men and women who are seen as having taken control of their destiny, who aren't afraid to step forward and stand apart from the crowd to take a firm position. In the face of big business and big government, we respect individuals who take charge of their everyday lives . . . because we hope to be able to do the same.

Culture has thus far been associated with an entire society. Yet even the smallest social settings can develop a shared set of rules for behavior—that is, a culture. In "Elevator Culture," I discuss the "proper" way to behave in an elevator when riding with other passengers. Surprisingly, perhaps, it turns out that elevator culture permits very little positive guidance for behavior—in fact, there may be only one socially correct way to stand in an elevator. No wonder some people prefer to take the stairs!

Before turning to the "snapshots" of culture in this first section of the book, let's return for a moment to the situation of having a number of international students in the small seminar that I teach. In introducing this section of the book, I emphasized the communication problems posed by my students' lack of familiarity with American culture. What I failed to stress, however, was that their presence in my seminar also had an important *positive* impact by bringing to bear on our classroom discussions the experiences of the diverse cultures they represented. In some cases, students from other countries added to our discussions by reinforcing the universal validity of our sociological generalizations. Their own experiences suggested that what was true about American society might also apply to their homelands. In other cases, however, my students added a cautionary input. Based on their experiences, certain relationships discussed in our class could probably not be generalized beyond American, or perhaps Western, culture. As a sociologist, I can safely say that I learned a great deal from being immersed, even if only on a secondhand basis, in cultures from around the world. ■

The Immaculate Americans

Being Cleaner Doesn't Mean We're Better

Body odor is big business. Every year, we immaculate Americans spend more money on deodorants and mouthwashes than we contribute to the United Way. In addition, we probably pass more time scrubbing, washing, spraying, bathing, squirting, and gargling than any other people in the history of the world. Every American, in fact, learns from an early age that cleanliness is considered next to Godliness—a sign that an individual is morally pure and sinless. No wonder Americans spend more than 1 billion dollars annually on soap—it's part of our culture.

In other parts of the world, however, we are regarded as neurotically concerned with our personal cleanliness. In some European countries, for example, American tourists are easily identified by their demands for a room with a private bath. Meanwhile, their European counterparts more often stay in rooms where they wash up daily in a small sink and take their baths down the hall. In their own countries, anyone caught showering twice a day would probably be regarded as either eccentric or ill.

Notwithstanding our present-day preoccupation, Americans can hardly take credit (*or* blame) for inventing a concern for cleanliness. Arab intermediaries, in arranging a marriage, sometimes rejected a prospective bride who didn't "smell nice." Sniffing and nose kissing have long been practiced by Eskimos, Philippine Islanders, and Samoans who recognized the desire for a pleasant odor. And bathing for purification is an ancient custom practiced by the early Hebrews, Muslims, and Hindus.

Medieval royalty even took baths, but only on occasion. In England, for example, King John bathed three times a year, always before a major religious festival. But church authorities and medical practitioners in the Middle Ages generally frowned on bathing, denying the general population access to the few existing baths. Instead, medieval people stuffed their nostrils with strong perfumes to disinfect the air and reduce the onslaught of black plague. Even after the Middle Ages, Queen Elizabeth I of England bathed only monthly (whether she needed it or not).

Major efforts to overcome the problem of personal cleanliness for the masses really weren't made until the mid-19th century. During the Industrial Revolution, the British were the plumbing pioneers. For those who lacked private facilities, the state built public bathhouses consisting of individual bathrooms with centrally controlled plumbing. By the early part of the 20th century, however, cultural diffusion had taken effect, and America had taken the lead in developing private bathrooms for the majority of citizens. For the first time in history, the home bathroom was no longer viewed as a status symbol but was regarded as a middle-class necessity.

Of course, everything is relative when it comes to culture, and some Americans have acquired such lofty cultural standards today that they think foreigners smell. Perhaps they are right, at least when judged by a national norm that refuses to tolerate any body odor at all. The odorous outsiders (who, by the way, probably smell pretty much like human beings are intended to) are then regarded by some Americans as dirty, slovenly, or perhaps even morally impure.

The bias is not new. Odor has often been used to discredit entire groups of people. During the Middle Ages, for example, European Jews were widely believed to have drunk the blood of Christian children as part of the Passover ritual to rid themselves of an "odor of evil." It was also rumored that after their conversion to Christianity, the Jewish malodor miraculously disappeared.

Closer to home, American blacks, Latinos, Hawaiians, and Native Americans have all been stereotyped in cultural images at one time or another as smelling different. And one of the most offensive olfactory images is that of elderly citizens—especially nursing home residents—who are too often stereotyped as reeking from incontinence, indifference, and the ravages of age.

Just how accurate are such cultural images of group differences in odor? Is it possible that the members of different ethnic and racial groups really do have distinctive smells? Consider, for example, the possible effect on the quality and quantity of perspiration of dietary differences or of jobs requiring strenuous physical activity. Such differences do vary by group; they might even differ by ethnicity or social class. Yet the perception of such group differences in odor seems entirely out of proportion to their actual occurrence, if they happen at all.

More likely, the charge of minority malodor is needed by bigots who are eager to justify discriminatory treatment against a group of people by dehumanizing them. The reasoning is simple enough: Animals, not human beings, give off a stench. Human beings must be treated according to the rules of civilized society; but animals can be mistreated, even slaughtered, at will. The members of group X give off a stench (they don't bathe and live like pigs); therefore, they can be mistreated.

The sociological question is answered best by recognizing that perception of odor is only one component in the much larger repertoire of cultural racism. Our beliefs about various groups are often supported by deeply rooted emotions acquired early that can linger throughout life. In the Jim Crow South, white Southerners had an intense emotional reaction to the possibility of desegregating their public facilities. Black skin was regarded almost as a contagious physical condition, something dirty that might rub off and contaminate those individuals who were fortunate enough to be white— hence, the need for norms requiring separate public conveniences that imply close contact, such as restaurants, theaters, buses, water fountains, and restrooms.

In his analysis of race relations in the United States, psychiatrist James Comer, himself a black American who overcame poverty and discrimination to become a well-known psychiatrist and author, recounts the story of a white teenage girl who was scolded by her father for having put a coin in her mouth. He yelled, "Get that money out of your mouth—it might have been in a nigger's hand!" His reaction reminds us of an important principle of human behavior: You really don't have to smell like a skunk to be treated like one! ∎

Baby Boomers
A Generation Without a Gap

Rock music has long been a symbol of adolescent rebellion. The "greasers" of the 1950s wouldn't have been caught dead listening to recordings of Glenn Miller, Woody Herman, or any other musician reminiscent of their parents' day. Similarly, members of the 1960s hip generation were too intent on distancing themselves from what they saw as oppressive traditional authority to regard tunes by Fats Domino and Chuck Berry with more than historical curiosity.

That's why it is so intriguing that today's high school and college students don't reject—and, in fact, embrace—the popular music of yesteryear. Of course, they still identify with the superstar songsters of their own age—Boyz II Men, Marky Mark, Motley Crüe, Bon Jovi, and the like. But amazingly, they also admire longtime rock idols of the 1960s and early 1970s who are now well into what we euphemistically call the "prime of life," otherwise known as middle age. During the past few years, oldsters such as Pink Floyd, Fleetwood Mac, Aerosmith, Carly Simon, the Grateful Dead, Mick Jagger, Van Morrison, Bonnie Raitt, George Harrison, and Paul Simon have all had top-selling albums. Simon's Grammy-winning album *Graceland* was the top-ranked compact disc just a few years ago. And according to *Billboard Magazine*, among the top concert moneymakers of 1992 were middle-agers Billy Joel, Bob Seger, and David Bowie. During the same period, concerts by 1960s oldies legends like 51-year-old Gene Pitney and Shirley Alston Reeves, former lead singer of the Shirelles, provoked sellout crowds. In 1994, the top concert draws continued to include an overrepresentation of middle-agers like the Rolling Stones, Pink Floyd, Billy Joel, Barbra Streisand, Elton John, Phil Collins, and the Grateful Dead.

Part of the continuing popularity of the 1960s rock stars is their nostalgic appeal to the moving human population explosion we now call the baby boomers, 76 million American men and women who were born between 1946 and 1964. Many of them were just coming of age during the 1960s as the Beatles, Rolling Stones, and Bob Dylan entered the music scene or later as Woodstock launched their generation into the 1970s. Even as their oldest members now approach their late 40s, the baby boomers wax nostalgic. They have glowing memories of the formative period in their lives and the music that it spawned.

Across the country, popular radio stations have now capitalized on this wave of nostalgia by airing programs that feature 1960s golden oldies or by sprinkling *Big Chill* hits throughout their otherwise contemporary format. But it isn't only nostalgic baby boomers who crave the sounds of the 1960s; their younger brothers and sisters and in some cases their children also do—and in a big way. Recently, for example, the weather vane of adolescent opinion, *Teen Magazine,* reported the results of a survey of its readers' favorite entertainers. Among the names of current idols in the entertainment world, such as Justine Bateman, Whitney Houston, Madonna, and Bon Jovi, were names associated with a previous generation, many of whom are 20, even 30 years older than their teenybopper fans—Kenny Rogers, Alabama, Bill Cosby, the Judds, and Cybill Shepherd. Similarly, a 1992 poll of the youthful audience for a popular MTV all-request music program named *Heart and Soul* by the Monkees as its top video of the year and 42-year-old Davy Jones as its choice for "cutest guy." Even more shocking, senior citizen singers Frank Sinatra and Tony Bennett have made spectacular comebacks, enjoying popularity even in the teenage music market.

Music is only one example of the baby boomers' immense and continuing cultural clout. During the 1960s, long before they were given a label, today's baby boomers had not only large numbers (half the population of the United States was under 25) but also plenty of disposable income. And they often disposed of it on 35mm single-lens reflex cameras, stereo components, bell-bottom jeans, mini-skirts, Hula Hoops, and so on. Business interests were, of course, thoroughly pleased with such free-spending habits. So pleased, in fact, that commercials such as the Oil of Olay ads promised that you wouldn't look "over 25!" And in his best-selling work, *The Greening of America,* law professor Charles Reich raised the possibility that our entire society would soon be transformed in the image of youthful hippies of the day.

During the closing years of the 1960s, there was reason to make such a prediction. The baby boomers were role models for everyone who emulated their teenage children's appearance. Middle-aged women donned bell-bottom jeans, tie-dyed shirts, sandals, and peace beads, while their husbands wore their hair shoulder length, their ties psychedelic, and their sideburns to the end of their ear lobes. Many also grew beards and mustaches to lengths that today would be regarded as thoroughly outrageous. Indeed, the style of the day was the style of the baby boomer generation: It seemed as if everybody was either young or wanted to be.

Although in the 1990s the baby boomers have just begun to reach midlife, they have lost none of their cultural clout. Just as they were trendsetters as youths, so they are now setting trends as adults. The baby boomers still boast large numbers and still spend lots of money. Of course, their consumer habits have changed with age and the times; they now buy VCRs, microwave ovens, compact disc players, and personal computers. But the fact that they continue to consume is enough to explain why so many midlife models are appearing in ads and commercials.

Moreover, notwithstanding the efforts of fashion designers, few women today actually feel obligated to wear the miniskirts of a younger generation. Instead, high school and college students often follow their parents' lead by adding to their formfitting wardrobe the loose-fitting styles formerly associated with middle age. The more youthful punk movement may have affected trends in new-wave fashion, art, and music; but their small numbers and limited purchasing power pretty much assured that punk style would not influence older generations.

Will the cultural clout of baby boomers persist into old age? Will they continue to set trends in music, art, and fashion in their 60s and 70s? They will, of course, still have large numbers on their side. By the year 2025, when the baby boomers achieve senior citizenship, more than 20% of the population will be over 65. Yet it is a sad truth that numbers alone are as likely to assure poverty as power. In fact, elder Americans living 200 years ago commanded much greater respect and privilege than they do today, despite (or perhaps because of) the fact that only 10% of the population lived to celebrate their 60th birthday. Granted, this figure is skewed somewhat by high rates of infant mortality. Nonetheless, under Puritanism, old age was regarded as a sign of election and a special gift from God. But when longevity increased and more sizable numbers of people survived to old age, the cultural clout of elders declined. Specifically, preferential seating arrangements in public vehicles for older people were abolished, mandatory retirement laws appeared, youthful fashions were preferred, and eldest sons lost their inheritance advantages.

More than sheer numbers, then, graying baby boomers of the future will need to maintain the free-spending habits that endeared them to commercial interests if they are to maintain their cultural clout. Not only will they need plenty of money, but they must be willing to spend it as they did in the past. If they are anything like previous generations of older Americans, however, this may not be realistic. Senior citizens tend to become "economy conscious" by reducing their use of credit and by shopping for price. Even if many baby boomers refuse to retire at 65 or 70, they will likely decide to temper their consumerism in favor of preparing for an uncertain future in terms of health care, economic depression, inflation, and the like. Depending on the course of public policy over the next few decades, even financially secure individuals may become quite conservative in their spending habits. This does not mean that aging baby boomers will be asked to live in poverty, only that they may be forced to give up their place as the cultural kingpins of American society. ∎

Hate Crimes Against Women
Being as Nasty as They Want to Be

Bigotry is making a comeback. Americans now tolerate forms of prejudice and discrimination that a decade ago would have been unthinkable. What in 1969 or 1974 might have been whispered behind closed doors is today more readily expressed in public; what was once considered taboo is now more socially acceptable to say even among total strangers. During the past few years, we have generated a *culture of hate,* in which bigotry finds legitimacy.

Women have often been a target of that hate. Andrew Dice Clay has made the art of slurring women a specialty. When Clay last hosted *Saturday Night Live,* a cast member and a popular singer—both women—refused to perform on that show, claiming that the comic's appearance would legitimize the ravings of "a hate monger."

At the same time, rock idol Madonna, who brought us such controversial classics as "Like a Virgin" and "Like a Prayer," has more recently extolled the pleasures of being spanked by men in a little number titled "Hanky Panky." Popular rappers such as Ice-T and NWA (Niggas With Attitude) express a violent sexual theme based on the view that "women are only asking for it anyway."

At Syracuse University, sociologist Gary Spencer recently studied the growth of JAP (Jewish American Princess) jokes on campuses around the country. He concluded that these jokes undoubtedly contain an element of sexism. In their more benign form, JAP jokes depict Jewish women as greedy and materialistic. But even more sinister versions suggest that the world would be better off if all Jewish females were eliminated: "A solution to the JAP problem: When they go to get nose jobs, tie their tubes as well."

A part of the culture of hate is the portrayal of women as victims of grotesque forms of violence in motion pictures that are ostensibly "meant" for an adult audience but that appeal to teenagers. The R-rated "slasher" films depict the torture, assault, and murder of women, with obvious sexual significance. In *Tool Box Murders,* for example, a "glassy-eyed lunatic" type is shown in a grotesque act of violence against a young woman while romantic music plays softly in the background. Such films undoubtedly lead some into believing that sex and violence are inseparable, that you cannot or should not have one without the other. Edward Donnerstein and his colleagues (1987) have concluded that a heavy diet of slasher movies can make some men more accepting of sexual violence against women. The danger of "imminent violence" might allow censorship of such movies without violating First Amendment freedoms, but few now contemplate this.

The FBI is keeping track of a growing phenomenon that it calls "hate crimes." These are criminal acts (either against property or persons) that are aimed at individuals because they are members of a particular group. Those directed against women because they are women are on the rise.

Of course, not all attacks against females can be regarded as hate crimes. Many are motivated by the relationship of the individuals involved. The murder of suburbanite Carol Stuart, allegedly by her husband, in October 1989, was apparently motivated by greed, the hatred of one individual for another, or both. It cannot be argued that Carol Stuart was an interchangeable victim; she was apparently chosen because of her relationship with her assailant.

But hate crimes are usually perpetrated against total strangers. Therefore, everyone in a particular group is a potential target. Moreover, when an assault is involved, it is usually a brutal attack carried out by several offenders who frequently injure their victim sufficiently to require hospitalization.

The case of the "Central Park jogger" has all of these elements. In April 1989, a gang of teenage thugs, allegedly shouting, "Let's get a woman jogger," ambushed, beat, and then raped a 28-year-old woman as she ran through Central Park after dark. Her attackers pelted her with rocks, smashed her with their fists and a metal pipe, and then left her for dead. For 13 days, she lay hospitalized in a comatose state suffering from a fractured skull, brain injury, and disfiguring cuts and bruises. The Central Park jogger just happened to be in the wrong place at the wrong time. Any other female jogger would have been similarly at risk.

Clearly, antifemale attitudes did not develop overnight. Just like other aspects of culture, prejudice against women has been around for many generations—actually, for centuries. Also, as a cultural phenomenon, antifemale attitudes are learned early in life, transmitted through the teachings of parents, siblings, friends, teachers, children's books, and television programs. By the time children are 5 years old, they already know the "proper" behavior in the gender roles they are expected to play. Recognizing their advantaged position, young boys often refuse to cross the gender lines and play with their sister's dolls. By contrast, girls are more willing to take the leap across genders—they frequently see their predicament and are less averse to playing with their brothers' trucks and guns.

It should also be emphasized that the culture of hate is in no way confined only to music, humor, and motion pictures. There are many men who hold women responsible for eroding their economic position in society. Most are able to express their hatred vicariously in a manner that, however disgusting, is not illegal—by telling a JAP joke at a party, laughing at an Andrew Dice Clay concert, "getting into" an R-rated slasher film on their VCRs, or parroting the lyrics of a hit record.

But some men become violent. Serial killers such as Ted Bundy, Son of Sam, the Hillside Strangler, and the Green River Killer all targeted women as their primary victims. In December 1989, a resentful young man took his semiautomatic rifle into the engineering college at the University of Montreal to get even with the "feminists" he claimed were responsible for his failures in life. In slaughtering 14 female engineering students, Marc Lepine blamed women for his failed relationships, low-paying jobs, and lack of education. Engineering, he reasoned, was a masculine occupation, from which women must be excluded. Instead, the director of admissions at the University of Montreal had denied him admission to its engineering program and that was "the last straw."

If we are serious about reducing violence against women, we must be willing to mount an assault against those aspects of our culture that legitimize the expression of anger and resentment against an entire group or category of people. In short, we should try to transform the culture of hate into a culture of compassion and tolerance. ∎

The Demise of Bystander Apathy
We Admire Idols of Activism

In 1964, in a now classic case, Kitty Genovese was stabbed to death in the middle of the night while 38 of her neighbors listened from the safety of their apartments. Although the victim screamed for help and her assailant took almost 30 minutes to kill her, no one even reported the incident to the police, never mind fight off Genovese's killer.

Social scientists of the day argued that this apparent indifference was a result of what they called "diffusion of responsibility." That is, although they may have been concerned for the victim, Genovese's neighbors also felt a lack of personal responsibility to intervene. They reasoned, "Why should I risk my neck when there are other witnesses who will surely come to the rescue?"

However it was explained at the time, the Genovese case was the first nationally recognized episode of bystander apathy—one of the most distasteful by-products of the American preoccupation with spectatorship. Although it was first acknowledged then, however, bystander apathy is a phenomenon not peculiar to the 1960s; nor is it exclusive to any one generation of people. Just by going through recent newspaper stories, it would not be difficult to argue that people still do not help one another.

Take the Manchester, New Hampshire woman who was brutally raped in a yard just steps away from her apartment. Apparently, she was in full view of several of her neighbors but they ignored her pleas for help. In Raleigh, North Carolina, a motorcyclist injured in an accident lay facedown on a crowded highway and counted 900 cars over a 3-hour period before anyone stopped to assist him. In Boston, a third-year medical student was jumped by four teenagers while riding his bicycle home from the hospital. Many people watched, but none of them intervened. In New York City, a group of jeering and joking youths watched while a 30-year-old man was electrocuted on the third rail of the subway station at Times Square. And on and on.

Observers of the social scene have used such cases in arguing for the existence of a destructive and callous side of human nature. Based in part on the writings of Freud and, more recently, of ethnologists such as Konrad Lorenz who emphasize the evolutionary basis for aggressive behavior, they have focused on bystander apathy to illustrate how people are moving away from one another. This point of view is sometimes so thoroughly one-sided, however, that it ignores the fact that altruism is a value in virtually all human societies and forms the basis for most of the world's great religions. Americans have long institutionalized altruism by awarding medals for outstanding acts of selfless heroism as, for example, in the medals awarded by the Carnegie Hero Fund Commission or, during wartime, in the U.S. Armed Forces' awarding of the Congressional Medal of Honor.

While some observers dwell on the seedier side of human nature, hundreds of others donate one of their kidneys for transplantation into another human being. Thousands more have donated their blood at some personal expense and inconvenience. And millions regularly donate money to their favorite charities.

Today, more than 30 years after the Genovese case, these acts of generosity and selflessness seem more abundant than ever. In addition, there seems to be less tolerance for those individuals who respond to others with indifference or selfishness. In fact, bystander apathy seems fast becoming the exception to what may be a new norm of social life: being willing to risk inconvenience, embarrassment, and even personal safety to come to the rescue of the victims of crimes and accidents. The evidence is, at this point, admittedly anecdotal and informal, but it is nonetheless highly suggestive. There have been numerous reports recently of acts of great heroism and courage performed by average citizens who haven't otherwise stood apart as paragons of virtue. The members of this breed of Good Samaritans are very serious about taking personal responsibility for the plight of others, refusing to take refuge in the anonymity of the crowd or the masses.

We used to hear about airliners being hijacked; now we also hear about passengers on a flight who overpower and subdue a potential hijacker. We used to see purse snatchers and muggers; now we also see bystanders who chase and catch the mugger. We used to read about physicians who drive past automobile accidents because of the fear of a lawsuit; now we also read about doctors who come to the rescue of accident victims and, in the process, may suffer injuries of their own. We used to see corruption in government and industry; now we also see "whistle-blowers" who risk being fired to expose practices that they believe to be dangerous to the public.

An example of personal altruism is the behavior of Lennie Skutnik, the young man who was honored by ex-President Reagan in 1982 for his heroic rescue of a survivor of an Air Florida crash in the icy waters of the Potomac River.

In 1986, Richard Young, a New York City fireman, risked serious injury to rescue a total stranger—a truck driver who hung by his arms from the steering wheel of the cab of his truck as it dangled over the edge of a bridge. Arriving on the scene, Young threw himself under the truck driver's body to break his fall. In saving the man's life, Young received a broken leg, a broken ankle, and severe back injuries.

In 1987, a 23-year-old Vietnamese immigrant went on a shooting spree through the streets of a major city, killing five persons and wounding two others before ending his own life. More of the wounded might have succumbed to their injuries if it hadn't been for the selfless efforts of two young people who came forward under gunfire to move victims from the street to an ambulance.

In 1991, two armed robbers on the run from the police were followed by John Amato, an alert ex-cop who was listening to a description of their getaway car on his police scanner. At great personal risk, Amato tailed the two suspects—even though they had spotted him—and kept the police informed over his cellular phone. Thanks to him, the two robbers were eventually arrested and charged with armed robbery.

In 1992, a small plane crashed into a small, ice-covered pond, injuring its student pilot and his flight instructor. The duo might have died were it not for the heroic efforts of two passersby who rushed out to the sinking plane and rescued the two with a ladder they had laid on the ice. One of the rescuers, David Leal, suffered a dislocated shoulder and hypothermia in the process.

In 1994, Jennifer Harbury, a young woman who was educated in the United States, staged a 32-day hunger strike in Guatemala City to dramatize the absence of human rights there and to demand information about her missing husband. As a result, the Guatemalan government immediately charged Harbury for making false accusations against the Guatemalan army. On Human Rights Day in Boston, Rigoberta Menshu, herself a winner of the Nobel Prize for Peace, defended and praised Harbury for her humanitarian efforts on behalf of the people of Guatemala.

In 1994, 15-year-old Razeena Sadiq was on her way to school when she spotted an apartment building in flames. Without regard for her own safety, Sadiq raced into the burning building four times—at one point crawling on her hands and knees through the smoke-filled corridors—to guide 13 residents to safety. Afterward, she gave her coat to a half-naked man whom she had rescued and then pounded on doors until she found him a place to escape the early-morning cold.

What characteristics distinguish these Good Samaritans from the rest of humanity? Social scientists have discovered that individuals who intervene in a dangerous situation are likely to have had training in first aid, lifesaving, or police work. In addition, they tend to be exceptionally tall and heavy. These attributes give them the sense of competence or efficiency—through training and strength—necessary to be injected into potentially hazardous situations. Good Samaritans also tend to be adventurous types who have taken other risks with their personal safety.

The most important conditions accounting for the rise of the Good Samaritan may be found in the types of heroes they choose to emulate. Researchers have discovered a common factor among German Christians, who during World War II, helped rescue the victims of their Nazi persecutors; civil rights activists of the 1950s and 1960s (called Freedom Riders); and altruistic children: the presence of someone to serve as a model of altruism. In the case of a child, that model is likely to be an intensely moralistic parent with whom the Good Samaritan can closely identify. In adults, models for appropriate behavior are also found in the national heroes they choose to emulate.

On the national level, we continue to have our idols of consumption—those bigger-than-life images on the screen, tube, or field of play, whose accomplishments fill our leisure hours with music, comedy, and drama. But there is now a new breed of national hero as well. Today, we have idols of activism—individuals who are admired and revered not for their ability to keep us entertained but for their courage to take active charge of their own lives and the lives of others. In the face of overwhelming and impersonal social, political, and economic forces, such as the threat of nuclear war, big government, and corporate mergers, we feel increasing admiration for those who come forward from their place among the spectators. This change in our culture may have made heroes out of the likes of Oliver

North, Bernard Goetz, the Guardian Angels, Sylvester Stallone as Rambo and Rocky, Dustin Hoffman in the film *Hero,* Charles Bronson in *Death Wish,* and Jeff Bridges in *Fearless;* but it has still made us admire the courage of Lennie Skutnick and Razeena Sadiq. ∎

Elevator Culture
You Really Can't Do Anything Else but Stare at the Door

Social psychologists conducted an experiment in which they gave elevator riders at Ohio State University an opportunity to help themselves to a coupon good for a complementary Quarter Pounder with cheese. After entering the elevator, riders saw a poster reading "Free McDonald's Burger" and a pocket underneath it in which coupons for one Quarter Pounder were located. All they had to do was take one.

Fifty-six people entered the elevator alone. Of this number, 26 were randomly permitted to ride without other passengers, while 16 rode with one other passenger and 14 rode with two other passengers (all of the "other passengers" were really confederates of the experimenters who decided on a random basis whether subjects rode with 2, 1, or no other riders).

Results obtained in this experiment showed that individuals riding alone were much more likely to help themselves to a coupon for a cheeseburger than were riders in the presence of other passengers. In fact, of those individuals riding by themselves, 81% took a free coupon. With one other passenger present, however, only 38% took a coupon; and with two other passengers present, only 14% helped themselves to a coupon.

Why would elevator passengers avoid doing something to their advantage—taking a coupon for a free cheeseburger—just because other riders were present? The answer seems to involve the influence of *elevator culture*—a set of unspoken, unwritten rules of behavior that are widely shared and generally observed by people in elevators who ride with other passengers. The riders in this experiment were eager to avoid doing something that might call attention to themselves in the public setting of the elevator, even if it meant sacrificing a free fast-food lunch. They didn't want to be deviant; they desired to avoid being embarrassed; they didn't want to look different.

Actually, there isn't very much you can do that is right in an elevator, especially if you are among strangers. Almost all of the rules of elevator riding seem to be *proscriptive*—things you are definitely not supposed to do. The only prescriptive—positive—rule involves standing quietly while facing the elevator door, and that is precisely what most passengers will do. Unless they want to be regarded as weirdos, most riders avoid talking to anyone they don't know, staring at anyone, touching anyone, even breathing on anyone (they wouldn't want to violate the personal space of other riders, even in a crowded elevator).

One interesting thing about elevator culture is that it extends far beyond the elevator walls. Actually, almost any public setting—whether walking on the streets of a city, eating in a restaurant, or sitting in the park—carries a set of rules that severely limit the quality and quantity of social interaction: In all of these places, there is little, if any, talking to, touching, or even looking at strangers. As a result, strangers in a big city who are physically close might as well be miles apart, as far as interaction is concerned.

Of course, individuals also have some control over their culture; they don't passively have to conform to it. In an early study of conformity, Solomon Asch (1952) studied a group of eight people, in a classroom situation, who were asked to match the length of a line drawn on the blackboard with one of three comparison lines drawn on an index card. All judgments were made out loud and in order of seating in the room. Actually, only one participant in the Asch study was a naive subject; and he voiced his judgment after hearing several other "students" state theirs first. (These others were confederates of Asch who had been instructed to respond incorrectly when asked to match the length of the lines.)

Over a number of trials with different groups, approximately one third of the naive subjects made incorrect estimates in the direction of the inaccurate majority—in other words, about one in three conformed. But when a lone dissenter gave support to the naive subject by going against the majority judgment, the rate of conformity dropped dramatically to less than 6%.

Thus, if even one person waiting in line for a table in a restaurant starts talking to other customers, he or she might serve as a role model for other customers to imitate. Who knows, maybe lots of people will take a chance and get involved in the conversation. And if one rider in a crowded elevator has the courage to take a coupon for a free cheeseburger, everybody might conceivably end up having lunch on McDonald's. ∎

Many of the ideas and evidence found in "The Immaculate Americans" were based on Gale Largey and David Watson's excellent 1972 article, "The Sociology of Odors," in *American Journal of Sociology*. In this article, Largey and Watson make a very strong case that olfactory sensitivities vary from culture to culture. The use of images of odor to discredit a group of people is only one form of dehumanization. For a fascinating examination of this phenomenon, see Sam Keen's *Faces of the Enemy: Reflections of the Hostile Imagination* (1986).

Evidence for the tremendous influence of "Baby Boomers: A Generation Without a Gap" can be found in *Great Expectations: America and the Baby Boom Generation* (1980) by Landon Y. Jones. To focus specifically on women at the leading edge of the baby boom generation, I recommend Winifred Breines's excellent book, *Young, White, and Miserable: Growing Up Female in the Fifties* (1992). For a cultural-materialist view of social customs more generally, read Marvin Harris's fascinating work, *Cultural Materialism* (1979). Harris suggests that the variety of cultural behavior around the world is a result of the adaptations that societies make to their particular environments. For example, in 1487, the Aztecs suffered from a profound shortage of animal protein in their diet; they were not able to raise cattle, sheep, goats, horses, pigs, or llamas. In response, they continued to incorporate cannibalism into their warfare. After a battle, they would eat their enemies—thousands of them—as an alternative source of animal protein.

Concerning "Hate Crimes Against Women," my colleague Jack McDevitt and I wrote *Hate Crimes: The Rising Tide of Bigotry and Bloodshed* (1993). In our research, we emphasize the cultural basis for violence directed against individuals based on their group membership—because of their race, gender, religion, national origin, or sexual orientation. The "culture of hate" seems to be implicated especially in "thrill hate crimes"—acts of violence committed for "the fun of it" by young people who don't fit well into society and are intensely angry. Susan Faludi's work *Backlash: The Undeclared War Against American Women* (1991) focuses specifically on many of the obstacles to women's equality as reflected in forms of popular culture such as television, fashion, and motion pictures.

The trend toward activist cultural heroes as introduced in "The Demise of Bystander Apathy" is beginning to show up in the sociological literature. For example, Myron Peretz Glazer and Penina Migdal Glazer, in their important book *The Whistleblowers: Exposing Corruption in Government and Industry* (1989) have studied the growing phenomenon of ethical resisters—those courageous workers who expose corruption in high places. Despite harassment and a strong possibility of defeat, these whistle-blowers operate out of a sense of moral responsibility to challenge the status quo. If you are interested in learning more about altruism and empathy in everyday life, read Alfie Kohn's book, *The Brighter Side of Human Nature* (1990). He convincingly presents evidence from sociology, psychology, and biology to suggest that human beings are more caring and generous than we give ourselves credit for. According to Kohn, helping others occurs as often as hurting others. Samuel Oliner and Pearl Oliner's penetrating work *The Altruistic Personality* (1988) examines hundreds of individuals who helped rescue victims of the Nazis during Hitler's reign of power. The Oliners emphasize that the rescuers had a deep-rooted empathy for other people's problems that they developed in their childhood homes. Their parents were profoundly moral individuals who often acted on their beliefs—in our terms, they were everyday versions of idols of activism.

A work by Robert Bellah, Richard Madsen, William Sullivan, Ann Swidler, and Steven Tipton, *Habits of the Heart: Individualism and Commitment in American Life* (1985), analyzes both the tradition and the direction of our cultural values. According to Bellah et al., we have lost touch with our cultural commitment to community, in favor of a preoccupation with rugged individualism. In the process, we have ignored the very traditions that might help us today.

■ **DEVELOPING IDEAS** *About Culture*

1. Writing topic: Name five of your heroes from fields such as business, sports, entertainment, religion, and politics or from everyday life. Then write an essay in which you identify the particular cultural values reflected in their heroic accomplish-

ments. To start, consider whether they are idols of production, consumption, or activism.

2. Writing topic: We have seen how much cultural clout the baby boomers have had in American society. Thinking about music, art, comedy, and television, identify some of the contributions that *your* generation has made to American popular culture.

3. Research topic: Analyze the lyrics to three top-40 songs in which an angry message is expressed. Can you identify these lyrics with a culture of hate? Do you believe that song lyrics reflect or affect the values of audience members?

4. Research topic: Let's say you were a sociologist who was studying the culture of your campus. Construct a one-page questionnaire to identify some of the values and practices that are widely shared among the students at your college. Then give the questionnaire to a sample of students. (To get at how values operate in everyday life, you might want to ask questions such as how many hours a week your respondents spend doing things like studying, partying, watching TV, and so on. You might also ask them to rank order certain activities—getting good grades, having a date, being well liked, making lots of money—in terms of how important they are.)

5. Research topic: Pick up a recent issue of a supermarket tabloid— preferably the *National Enquirer* or the *Star*. Analyze all of the profiles in that issue with respect to the human qualities and problems that they emphasize. First, determine how many profiles feature celebrities. How many of these are entertainers, business leaders, or politicians? How many would you regard as idols of consumption? Next, find out how many profiles feature ordinary people who do extraordinary things. How many were Good Samaritans? How many performed miracles or great acts of courage? How many would you regard as idols of activism?

PART TWO

Socialization

It was a disquieting scene: three African Americans waiting for a bus, and, across the road, a young white child—he couldn't have been more than 2 or 3 years old—shouting racial slurs at the top of his lungs as he took bites from a Three Musketeers bar. Just as the trio got aboard the bus, the boy's mother rushed over, picked him up, and carried him away. At first, she was furious . . . that he had left her side without asking permission. But then she smiled as he continued to yell "nigger" and point in the direction of the bus as it sped away.

Just like the child at the bus stop, we aren't born knowing the content of our culture; we learn it. We absorb our culture—we learn love of country, motherhood, apple pie, and racism—through a process of interacting with others—parents, teachers, friends, television characters—that we call *socialization.*

In "Mapping Social Geography," we examine the sources of the *cognitive* elements in our culture—those aspects that give us basic information about reality. We also discover that our shared knowledge of what the world around us is like isn't always accurate. In fact, many of us have a distorted view of social reality. The effect of such distortions in our perception may be profound: Many of the decisions we make in everyday life are in part a result of what we believe the world to be like. If, for example, we exaggerate the likelihood of being a victim of violence, we might decide to carry a handgun. If we overestimate the wealth of our nation, we may oppose programs that aid the homeless.

Socialization is absolutely essential for individuals to become humanized members of their society. Without internalizing culture, we would all be "sociopaths"—essentially unsocialized individuals who lack conscience, human warmth, and empathy for the problems of other people. Yet just because individuals accept the values and norms of their group doesn't necessarily mean that they will automatically reject violence. Indeed, even the most brutal, most repulsive behaviors have been taught during the normal course of socialization.

"Foul Play in the Stands" suggests that, through their choice of games, some cultures actually promote the expression of aggressive behavior. Rather than serving as a "safety valve" for pent up hostility, watching players block, tackle, or punch out one another actually teaches spectators to become more, not less, aggressive. In some societies, where aggressive behavior is virtually absent from everyday interaction, combative sports simply do not exist. Such games have little appeal to the members of a society who socialize their youngsters to be cooperative and peaceful. But in warlike societies, combative contact sports, such as boxing and football, predominate—and, for good reason: They socialize individuals to accept the legitimacy of their violence. So much for the catharsis theory of aggression.

Any discussion of the way in which values are transmitted to the members of American society would be incomplete if it failed to include a discussion of the mass media. In particular, television has an immense influence as an *agent of socialization,* if for no other reason than that the average child spends 4 to 5 hours daily in front of the tube. I often hear concerned Americans voice their criticism of television for what it supposedly does to children. And much of this criticism is well deserved. But let's put the effect of television in perspective: There is far less street crime in Japan, yet Japanese television is even more violent than ours. Why? Perhaps because few Japanese parents use television as a baby-sitter. Instead, they sit *with their children while they watch the tube,* ready to monitor, interpret, and discuss. It isn't so much that American television is so strong but that our other institutions—family, business, religion, and schools—aren't doing their part that may be at the heart of the problems we now face.

Socialization does not come to an abrupt end just because someone grows up. To some degree, adults continue to change throughout life; and they, too, are very much influenced by what they watch on the tube. "Confessions of a Soap Opera Addict" suggests that the fantasy on TV is often seen as the reality. In the extreme case, soap opera *characters* become our "good friends." We may even send them gifts. In "Adult Socialization Can Be Murder," I examine an extreme example of development into adulthood gone awry—the case of murderers who don't start killing until they reach their 30s, 40s, or even 50s. I ask, If early childhood is really the critical factor, why didn't these killers begin their murder sprees when they were 12 or 18 or 24? Why did they wait until they were middle-aged adults?

To some extent, most Americans share an overall way of life. They accept at least some values and practices from the dominant culture as their own. At the same time, Americans are not rubber stamps of one another. Just as they share in the dominant culture, their worldviews are also colored by their being members of a *subculture*—a group whose members have their own peculiar set of values, objects, and practices. In "Sticks and Stones May Break . . . " we see the importance of membership in subcultures for establishing an individual's personal identity. The question, "Who am I?" is often answered in subcultural terms: "I am Irish American," "I am Latin American," and so forth. These subcultural names are important in symbolic terms for their ability to express the shared consciousness and pride of a group in society whose members may struggle with their subcultural identity.

Charles Horton Cooley, writing at the turn of the century, suggested that our self-image is developed through the "looking-glass process." That is, we form a sense of self by interacting with others. In this process, we come to make a judgment of our self—that we are smart, attractive, moral, and so forth—based on the judgments that others make of us. Thus, the other people in our lives are, in a sense, a mirror in which we see our own reflection. Cooley called the result of this process the *looking-glass self.*

If self-esteem develops in social interaction, then names can hurt you as much as sticks and stones. In "Sticks and Stones May Break . . . " we see that children who are given unpopular or unusual names may be treated in a negative way. In response, they develop poor self-esteem and actually behave as predicted: badly. The entire process becomes a "self-fulfilling prophecy."

When applied to a group of people, names often contain a cultural *stereotype*—an unflattering image that the members of a society learn from their parents, teachers, friends, and the mass media. The racial slur "nigger" shouted by the toddler in the bus stop scene that opened this section is "only" a name. But it contains one of the nastiest cultural stereotypes ever taught to our children.

The importance of the self can hardly be exaggerated. According to the California Task Force to Promote Self-Esteem and Personal and Social Responsibility, self-esteem is a "primary factor" affecting how well an individual functions in society. Many, if not most, of our major social problems, the California Task Force contends, originate in low self-esteem. It should be emphasized, at the same time, that the chain of cause and effect runs both ways—that self-esteem itself is affected very much by an individual's involvement in such social problems as poverty, domestic violence, and educational inequality. ■

Mapping Social Geography
Why We Create the World in Our Own Image

Ask Johnny to locate the United States on a world map and he might very well point to the continent of Africa or South America. In fact, according to a recent Gallup survey, 20% of Americans aged 18 to 24 can't identify their own country. When it comes to geographic knowledge, America's young people place last behind their counterparts from Mexico, Britain, France, Italy, Canada, Japan, West Germany, and Sweden.

To many, this lack of geographic knowledge is shocking. It shouldn't be as unacceptable as our ignorance of *social* geography, however. The truth is that many Americans have grown up with a distorted view of social reality. Even if they are able to distinguish the United States from Mexico or Canada, they don't realize, for example, that Caucasians are a minority among the world's racial groupings or that Christianity is a minority religion worldwide.

American parochialism can be easily demonstrated by questioning even the most sophisticated individuals about elementary social facts. For example, what percentage of the population of the United States is Jewish? Black? Catholic? Or what percentage of our population will be over 65 years of age by the year 2000?

I am always somewhat surprised when college students estimate that 30% of the population of the United States is Jewish (actually, the figure is close to 1.9%); that 40% of all Americans are black (the figure for those who regard themselves as black or African American is more like 13%); that 60% of our population is Catholic (the figure is 20% maximum); that 40% of our elders are in nursing homes (the figure is more like 4%).

Where does misinformation about our society come from? Why can't Americans seem to get their social facts straight? Part of the answer is that all of us are socialized with an unrepresentative sample of social reality. Inevitably, we learn to view the world from our own biased and limited slice of experience. We tend to apply what we see every day to what we don't see every day.

Consequently, given our tendency to separate our schools and neighborhoods by race, social class, religion, and age, it is not surprising that our generalizations are often inaccurate. A person socialized while growing up in Boston may come to believe that 60% of the population of the United States is Catholic because that is what he sees on his street, in his neighborhood, or at work. If the same person had grown up in Waco, Texas, he might instead believe that there were only two or three Catholics in the United States, if not the world. Similarly, people living in Washington, D.C. may well be convinced that 70% of all Americans are black; growing up in Vermont, their answer might be zero.

A second reason for our distorted view of social reality is that we usually don't validate or test our beliefs about society in any systematic way. We can go through a lifetime clinging to old stereotypes that are patently false, yet we wouldn't know the difference.

If Ivan Boesky is implicated in an insider trading scandal, some individuals will conclude that Boesky engaged in shady business practices *because* he is Jewish. If an Italian American makes headlines because he is a member of organized crime, many will remember that he is of Italian descent. If someone French does the same thing, we don't remember his ethnic identity at all because it seems irrelevant. Or we treat him as an exception that proves the rule.

A third reason for our misinformation about social reality involves our infatuation with television. Communication research conducted for more than a decade indicates that heavy television viewers tend to overestimate the percentage of the world population that is white and male, underestimate the amount of poverty in our country, and exaggerate the amount of violence they are likely to encounter. Heavy viewers also overestimate the proportion of jury trials in our courts and the number of miracle cures performed by doctors. They are socialized to accept a false view of social reality, because this is precisely what they see on TV every evening beginning at 8 p.m. The world of prime-time television is overpopulated by white males who possess more than their share of wealth and power. On dramatic series, defendants typically receive a jury trial and doctors routinely cure their patients. As noted in "Confessions of a Soap Opera Addict," many viewers do not distinguish the fantasy that they see portrayed on television from the real world. For them, television is the real world.

What difference does it make that so many Americans are socialized to accept a distorted view of social reality? That they operate on the basis of false stereotypes of what our society is like? That they are misinformed about other people and maybe about themselves?

The answer lies in the relationship between the way we define the world and the decisions we make about it.

For example, if we are mistakenly convinced that a majority of our citizens will be over 65 by the year 2020, we might decide to avoid national bankruptcy by reducing our commitment to Social Security for the elderly.

If Jews are mistakenly believed to make up 30% of our population, then the myth of a dominant Jewish presence in banking or the press sounds more plausible.

If we underestimate the amount of poverty existing in our country, then we might also vote down social programs for the poor and the homeless.

And if we exaggerate the amount of violence we are likely to encounter in everyday life, then we are also more likely to double lock our doors, buy a handgun, and support the death penalty. That is exactly what is happening right now: Firearms are increasingly available, and a majority of Americans favor the death penalty.

We can assume, I believe, that Johnny will continue to watch 4 or 5 hours of television daily and therefore continue to be socialized to the same unrealities depicted on the tube. In all probability, he will also maintain his segregated relationships in everyday life. What can we do, then, to assure that Johnny's perception of reality is not so far off the mark? The burden of responsibility, I believe, can be placed on our nation's classrooms.

One of the important functions of formal education is to broaden our personal experience, to serve as an agent of socialization with aspects of life that we might otherwise never experience firsthand—in a word, to clarify social reality. In our efforts to improve basic skills in English, mathematics, and geography, we must not forget to place equal emphasis on the skills necessary to good citizenship and humanitarianism. Young people need to be made aware of the existence of poverty and homelessness, flaws in the criminal justice system, prejudice and discrimination, and their own mortality. If our schools can teach Johnny to identify the United States on a world map, they can also teach Johnny that he is not at the center of the universe. ∎

Confessions of a Soap Opera Addict

The Daytime Serials Are More Than I Bargained For

I've been watching *Days of Our Lives* each day of my life for more than 25 years. It all started in 1968, when I took a year off to finish my doctoral dissertation. Each afternoon, my wife and I sat together in the living room of our small apartment: She watched soap operas; I wrote my thesis. Working at home was tough enough, and eaves-dropping on midday melodrama didn't help. In fact, it only rein-forced my long-held impression that soaps were at about the same intellectual level as Saturday morning cartoons—but these, at least, had action. Did anyone really care whether Julie and David got together again, when Marie would discover that her fiancé was actually her long-lost brother, or whether Missy was pregnant with "another man's" child?

I didn't think so. Soap operas were television's "opiate of the masses," I had decided: that medium through which too many Americans vicariously escaped their dreary existence into the make-believe world of the rich and beautiful. While the pressing economic and social problems of our society went ignored, millions of *General Hospital* groupies became Luke and Laura, if only for a few minutes a day. They needed that soap opera "fix" to make their lives seem exciting and worthwhile. America's daytime serial fanatics were being distracted from improving their own lives by a particularly insidious form of fantasy and escapism.

I was especially annoyed by the depiction of women. They seemed always to be getting pregnant, not for the purpose of having children but to manipulate and control the men in their lives. They used pregnancy to trap boyfriends into unwanted marriages or husbands into maintaining unwanted marriages. In addition, any woman who dared have a career in a field traditionally dominated by men—medi-cine, law, business—was either mentally ill or evil. The sex role socialization message was unmistakable: Women were to stay out of the boardrooms and executive offices and stay in the kitchens and bedrooms "where they belonged."

It occurred to me that, in some perverse way, soap operas were a mass form of socializing young people to accept the status quo. Even while college students of the 1980s were scheduling or skipping courses to accommodate *General Hospital,* the majority of daytime serial watchers were high school graduates who had never attended college, mostly middle-aged women. Many used the characters on soaps as role models for how to handle their spouses. But what they learned frightened me: first, that infidelity and promiscuity were acceptable, even desirable, modes of sexual behavior; second, that divorce was the answer to any difference, no matter how trivial. If your marriage wasn't smooth as glass, get a divorce. Or a lover. Better yet, get a lover, then a divorce.

By the third or fourth week of watching out of the corner of my eye, I noticed something peculiar was happening to me. If I had to be away during a weekday afternoon, I'd call home for a rundown of that day's episodes. I scheduled meetings with colleagues so I wouldn't miss a particular serial. It got to the point where my wife would have to tear me away from *my* show to take a phone call or answer the door. It was painful to admit, but I was hooked. I was brainwashed. I had become a socialized "soapie."

Perhaps as a sort of therapy, I spent a good part of the next few years immersed in the study of soap operas. It was legitimate: I was teaching a course in mass communication, and my students were discussing the impact of television on society. I read what the experts—psychologists, sociologists, and assorted communications specialists—had to say. I even assigned student projects to analyze the characters on daytime serials.

Surprising, to me at least, was their conclusion that soap operas were much better than prime-time dramatic series in representing women, minorities, and older people in central roles. While young and middle-aged males were vastly overrepresented on prime-time television, in soap operas one half of the characters were women. Even more to their credit, soap operas featured actors and actresses who remained on the show for decades. Many of them aged gracefully and remained thoroughly attractive, while they continued to play roles central to the plot. Indeed, older people were treated much better on soap operas than on most other television fare. And the daytime serials frequently focused on a range of social problems: intergroup conflict, juvenile delinquency, alcoholism, organized crime—issues that were all but ignored by soaps' prime-time counterparts.

It was soon clear to me why soaps are so appealing to so many. For one, they provide us with the things we find lacking in modern life. Monday through Friday, without fail (barring an occasional hijacking or a presidential news conference), we follow our "good friends" into their offices, living rooms, and bedrooms. We attend their weddings and funerals, visit them in the hospital after surgery or childbirth. We watch them argue with their spouses, make love with their mistresses, and punish their children. We often get to know more about the personal lives of our favorite soap opera characters than we know about our real neighbors. In an era of anonymity, soap operas give us intimacy. Sadly, for those who are socially isolated, this may be the one and only source of intimacy in their lives, but perhaps this is better than nothing.

Soap operas make us feel good about ourselves. Misery loves miserable company, and our own problems are somehow less painful when we're able to compare them with the troubles of those we admire. The world of the daytime serial is the world of the wealthy, beautiful, and powerful—our cultural heroes, the people we aspire to become. Yet these characters have problems with their families and friends, much worse than ours. So we feel better, at their expense, of course.

Soap opera intimacy often takes the form of snooping but only in the most positive sense. By eavesdropping, we're given the opportunity to rehearse our own emotional reactions to problems that may confront us in everyday life. Observing untimely deaths, kidnappings, divorces, and mental illness on television, we learn something about the manner in which we might handle similar problems in our own lives.

At least part of the influence of daytime serials can be attributed to the credibility of television as a form of mass communication. Study after study shows that Americans trust the authenticity of the images they see on the tube. In the process, however, heavy viewers often develop a distorted view of social reality. They tend to exaggerate, for example, the amount of violence they are likely to encounter in everyday life, the proportion of criminal cases that end in a jury trial, and the likelihood that physicians will perform miracle cures. For these viewers, the fantasy world on television becomes the reality. During the 5 years that Robert Young played Dr. Marcus Welby, the actor received more than 250,000 letters asking him for medical advice. Admiring fans were apparently unable to distinguish actor Young from character Welby.

This incredible power of soap operas as an agent of socialization was brought home to me several years ago when I met two longtime stars of *Days of Our Lives,* Susan and Bill Hayes (Doug and Julie). As an interested observer, I couldn't resist asking them the questions that might confirm what I always suspected: Do soap opera addicts confuse the fantasy world of the daytime serials with the real world in which they live? Yes—and often. Whenever a *Days of Our Lives* star either gives birth (it's only a pillow), gets married (a rhinestone wedding ring), or dies (usually a failure to renegotiate the actor's contract), cards and gifts appear at the studio, they said.

For me, soaps have a special appeal. As a sociologist, I investigate problems that have no easy solutions. I spend years studying serial killers, for example, and am troubled that we can't predict from childhood experience who will eventually commit hideous crimes. I research the causes of prejudice and discrimination and still see the number of racist acts of vandalism and desecration increasing. And like others, I see criminals too often get suspended sentences while their victims suffer; the rich get richer as homelessness grows; and the questionable ethics of politicians go unpunished.

And that's how soaps are different. Warm, friendly, predictable, they make sure people get what they deserve. ∎

Foul Play in the Stands

A Look at Sports Fan Aggression

I have always regarded my annual visit to Sullivan Stadium to see the New England Patriots as a form of recreation—in the same league as an evening at a comedy club or an afternoon dip in the pool. Apparently, however, not all football fans agree with me.

On a recent visit, in fact, I overheard two men extolling the virtues of professional football and boxing. In an increasingly loud and obnoxious conversation, they argued that football *was* important, if not essential. In their view, it serves as a "safety valve," an outlet for relieving our feelings of anger and hostility that might otherwise swell up inside and eventually burst in a bloody explosion of aggression and violence. According to these gentlemen, without combative contact sports, we would surely be at the mercy of our primal instincts, engaging in war with one another if not with most of the nations in the world.

If you've ever been to a professional football game, you might well agree that it does provide an arena for the fans to "let off steam." Spectators shout obscenities and racial slurs, scream at officials, and follow the cheerleaders in their ritualistic exhortation to "push 'em back, push 'em back, way back." During a lull in the action, it is not unheard of for fans to display their crazy mascots (for example, a bird, a bear, or a lion) or to hold up aggressively worded signs ("Cream the Colts," "Destroy the Dolphins," "Liquidate the Lions"). It is obvious that at least some of the fans vicariously participate in the game on the field of play. Maybe they even believe they are real football players.

Psychologists call this phenomenon "catharsis of aggression." They argue that spectators, by letting off steam at a hockey or football game, become less hostile, less angry, and less likely to be aggressive in the future. From this point of view, followers of football are also less apt to punch another person in the nose or go after someone with a knife. In societal terms, they may be less prone to attack the shoreline of a neighboring state, to drop bombs on civilians in other countries, or to go to war. And you thought that football was mere sport.

Catharsis of aggression may sound reasonable, but so did the Edsel until Ford Motor Company examined its sales figures. If fans really get more mellow and calm as a result of attending a combative contact sporting event, why do we read so much about violent outbursts or riots among spectators at boxing matches, soccer contests, and football games? In case you missed the headlines during the past few years, fans have been beaten, trampled, and even hacked to death with machetes at these events. And most of these brutal events in the stands followed outbursts of violence among the players. Apparently, the spectators imitated their heroes on the field of play.

Jeff Goldstein and Robert Arms, while professors at Temple University, studied the level of hostility among spectators at an Army-Navy football game in Philadelphia. In interviews with fans both before and after the contest, these two social psychologists discovered that spectator anger increased by watching the game, whereas the level of hostility among spectators attending a "control" gymnastic meet did not differ before and after the competition.

Maybe it's the beer. Perhaps spectators at football games would benefit from catharsis if only they didn't have so much to drink during the game. After all, alcohol does tend to weaken our inhibitions against expressing aggression. Or perhaps it's the kind of people who attend combative sporting events. Maybe football or hockey attracts Neanderthal types—individuals who are, by nature, already vicious and violent.

Robert Arms and his associates wondered the same thing, so they brought their own subjects—college students enrolled in a psychology course—to a sporting event. On a random basis, one third of their students attended a professional hockey contest, one third attended professional wrestling, and one third attended a swimming competition. All of them arrived together and were escorted to a spare dressing room. None was allowed to have any alcohol beverage. They were assigned to one or another of the sporting events regardless of whether or not they liked the particular sport.

So in this study, there was no beer and the Neanderthals were as likely to attend swimming as wrestling. Yet significant increases in hostility were registered among students who attended hockey and wrestling, but not among spectators assigned to observe swimming. Apparently, spectators become more hostile after observing an aggressive sporting contest, whether that aggression was realistic, as in football and hockey, or a spoof, as in professional wrestling. Final score: Imitation 2, Catharsis 0.

I suppose it still could be argued, regardless of the influence of contact sports on its fans, that these sports have a more general effect by "draining off" the aggression that would otherwise end in war and murder. If catharsis of aggression works in this way, however, wouldn't you think the murder rate would drop after a well-publicized boxing match? But when sociologist David Phillips examined the homicide rates in America immediately following televised heavyweight prize fights, he found a brief but sharp increase in homicides of 13%. This effect seemed to peak on the third day after the prize fights.

Years ago, anthropologist Richard Sipes (1973) examined another version of this argument by comparing societies classified as either warlike or peaceful. Now, if those in favor of football are correct and the sport really does "drain hostility," then we would expect combative contact sports to be common in peaceful societies but relatively scarce in warlike societies. Instead, Sipes found exactly the opposite. Members of warlike societies also loved football; members of peaceful societies weren't interested in it. Sipes concluded that combative sports could hardly be regarded as an alternative to war for the reduction of pent-up aggression. Rather, societies whose members are very aggressive in one area of life tend to be aggressive in other areas of life as well. Indeed, football and hockey may actually socialize youngsters to express aggressive behavior later in life, including preparing them for warfare. What better way for children to develop affection for winning than to incorporate competitive teamwork into their play?

I don't recall television, bowling, or bingo fanatics arguing that their favorite pastime saves us from ourselves. Can't lovers of football and hockey just admit that the violence on the field of play is exciting, entertaining, perhaps a diversion from their otherwise mundane lives, or even an excuse to get together with the boys? Surely, these are reasons enough to see professional athletes beat one another to a pulp. ∎

Sticks and Stones May Break . . .
In Reality, Names May Indeed Hurt You

What's in a name? Plenty, if you happen to be political spokesperson Larry Speakes, Professor Robert Smart, psychiatrist Ronald Bliss, or District Court Judge Darrell Outlaw. Whether or not such names inspired career choices, they undoubtedly have provided material for countless after-dinner conversations. Can't you imagine Dr. Bliss being ribbed about teaming with Dr. Ruth for a late-night advice show?

According to psychologist Ron Harre and his associates at State University of New York at Binghamton, and confirmed in countless other studies, the influence of names begins in childhood. Names that we are familiar with—common names, such as John and Michael—are associated with images of strength and competence, whereas unusual names, such as Ivan and Horace, conjure up weakness and passivity. Consequently, those kids who are unfortunate enough to have been given bizarre or unpopular names are sometimes poorly adjusted and pessimistic about their prospects of being successful in the future; they tend to score lower on achievement tests and get lower grades in school.

This phenomenon extends into adulthood. Men who have strange or unusual names are more likely to suffer from mental illness or to have criminal records. In many cases, a *self-fulfilling prophecy* may operate during the socialization process. A child is ridiculed because of his name. As a result, he develops a negative attitude toward himself that influences his behavior in the classroom and on the playground. And teachers and peers notice this poor behavior. They assume that kids with unusual names aren't very competent or skillful. So very little is seen, very little is expected, and very little is obtained.

The importance of names is nowhere more important than in Hollywood. Consider all the celebrities who weren't born with the right name for the image they want to portray. The former William Bailey is now Axl Rose; Alphonso D'Abrusso is Alan Alda; Robert Zimmerman calls himself Bob Dylan; Frances Gumm's stage name was Judy Garland; and Patricia Andrzejewski is better known as rock singer Pat Benetar.

The flip side of this is that uncommon names sometimes imply uniqueness. One might speculate that Zsa Zsa Gabor, Ya Hoo Serious, River Phoenix, Moon Zappa, Pee Wee Herman, Yakov Smirnoff, Rip Torn, Whoopi Goldberg, Mr. T, and Minnie Pearl owe at least part of their celebrity status to their names.

Minority groups are also painfully aware of the power of a name to socialize its members to failure and negative self-esteem. People of color prefer to be called *black* or *African American*. They reject labels such as *colored* and *Negro*, contending that they were long ago assigned to them by outsiders. Jesse Jackson recently called for the elimination of the black label in favor of a group identity such as *Afro-American* that would emphasize an African cultural heritage in the same way that white ethnic groups—Irish Americans, Polish Americans and Italian Americans—choose to stress their European ancestry. Even the term *minority* may be falling out of favor, as more and more people of color refuse to see themselves as playing a "minor" role in American society. Similarly, many women now resent being labeled *girls, babes,* and *chicks* because of the infantilized image. And older Americans tell survey researchers that they like being called *senior citizens* rather than *aged* or *elderly*, indicating that old age continues to be a difficult situation for millions.

People who possess a physical disability have often been victimized by harmful and misleading names. Given the negative connotation of the word *cripple*, it is clear why they seek to avoid being referred to in this way. But even the word *handicapped* is not always appropriate, deriving its meaning from an earlier period in which individuals with physical disabilities were forced to the streets, to beg, literally, cap in hand. There are numerous individuals today—blind, deaf, in wheelchairs, and on crutches—who actively seek to maximize their independence and who prefer not being labeled as handicapped.

By characterizing the entire person, the word *disabled* completely ignores the possibility that an individual might possess strengths as well as weaknesses. Yet very few persons are actually disabled in the absolute sense; most possess certain disabilities, some more severe than others, but they also have abilities that can be nurtured and developed if they are not overlooked. A paraplegic may never be able to run in the New York Marathon without the help of a wheelchair, but he or she may still become a brilliant lawyer or physician.

The symbolism in name-calling makes it just as dangerous as sticks and stones. Thousands change the name that appears on their birth certificate; thousands more drop an offensive middle name or use a nickname to avoid the negative attention provided by the formal version of their name. For minority groups, the painful history represented by a label often becomes part and parcel of the consciousness-raising rhetoric of their causes. Socialization counts a great deal: To accept the name is regarded as accepting the stereotyped image that group members have worked so hard to modify or overcome. Under such circumstances, the word may not be the thing, but it certainly has an effect that means the most—an individual or group's identity.

Whoever suggested that names will never hurt you must have been named John or Judy or maybe even Robert. It is doubtful that Horace or Eugene would have agreed. ∎

Adult Socialization Can Be Murder
Development Continues Throughout Life

Everything we have learned about the process of socialization suggests that what happens to us while we are very young is extremely important for shaping the rest of our lives. Suffering a horrible experience at the tender age of 2 can leave us with a lifelong phobia. Losing a loved one at 4 or 5 can contribute to making an individual into an emotionally needy adult. Failing the sixth grade can affect our self-image, even many years later.

Yet while early childhood may be critical, we must not forget that development continues throughout life. To focus only on the first few years in the biography of an individual may be to ignore some of the most influential aspects of his or her development.

Erik Erikson, for example, who was a student of Sigmund Freud and a famous theorist in his own right, proposed that the close personal relationships that are formed by an individual during young adulthood help determine a sense of intimacy. According to Erikson (1950), if such relationships are not successfully established, the individual will suffer a profound sense of isolation. What is more, in midlife (between the ages of 30 and 50), a failure to master the challenges of work and raising a family can result in an individual's coming to a nonproductive, egocentric sense of self.

To understand what can happen when adult socialization fails, we might examine its most extreme, most deadly consequences. It is interesting to note that most mass murderers—those who massacre large numbers of people—don't kill until they are middle-aged men—in their 30s, 40s, or even 50s. James Huberty, for example, who massacred 21 people, mostly Hispanic children, at a San Ysidro McDonald's, was 41; George Hennard, who opened fire in a Killeen, Texas cafeteria, killing 23, was 35; and R. Gene Simmons, who exterminated 14 members of his family in Russellville, Arkansas, was 46. If early childhood had been the critical factor, then these killers would probably have expressed their murderous impulses much earlier in life—say, by the time they were in their teens or early 20s.

Many mass killers do have profound problems growing up. They may have been abused, neglected, or even abandoned. But so have hundreds of thousands—perhaps even millions—of people who never kill anyone and who never will. The determining factor in the process of creating a mass murderer seems to reside in what happens to a killer when he attempts to make the transition into adulthood or even later. Does he have adequate support systems in place—family, friends, and neighbors—to get him through the tough times, to encourage and support him when he loses a job or an important relationship? Or is he set adrift to fend for himself in an unfamiliar and unfriendly world of anomie? In Erik Erikson's terms, does he suffer a profound sense of isolation at the very time in his life that he needs social support?

Also relevant is whether mass killers are successful at home and at work. Actually, most of them have suffered a number of losses in important areas of life—for example, the loss of a close relationship by separation or divorce or a profound financial loss through being fired or terminated. In Erikson's terms, having failed to master the challenges of work and raising a family, they feel a profound sense of stagnation. James Huberty, after losing his job, moved from a small town in Ohio to a suburb of San Diego. After settling in California, he again became unemployed. This time, however, his family and friends were back home in Ohio. He didn't have anyone to give him the psychological boost that he so much needed.

What happens (or fails to happen) in the biography of a mass murderer may give us clues as to what can be done to prevent violence in general, even when committed by otherwise unremarkable members of society. Of course, it would be wonderful if we were able to intervene in the early childhood of every individual who is in trouble. But we must also not ignore those troubled young people who are already in their teen years and beyond early intervention.

The majority of adult offenders do have a juvenile record, but the majority of teenagers with a juvenile record do not later become criminals. Many adolescents who commit deviant acts when they are 14 wouldn't dream of committing the same crimes when they reach 24 or 25. Just because we cannot reach troubled youngsters during the first few years doesn't mean that we should give up on them later. On the contrary, if Erikson is right, then we should be doing everything possible to help such teenagers over the obstacles of developing into adults so that they can become productive citizens. In the process, we might even prevent a mass murder. ∎

■ F O C U S *Suggestions for Further Reading*

As suggested in "Sticks and Stones May Break . . . ," labeling children with an unpopular name can sometimes become the basis for a self-fulfilling prophecy. They are expected to perform poorly, treated accordingly, and eventually come to perform as expected. For a discussion of the looking-glass self, you might read Charles H. Cooley (1902). I would, however, suggest that you first read the work of George Herbert Mead, a University of Chicago social philosopher whose insights into the development of the self continue to provide major direction for sociological research. Particularly germane is his discussion of *role taking*—the process whereby an individual learns to take another person's point of view. By means of role taking, children come to define themselves in the way that significant others (for example, mother and father) view them. If mommy and daddy see a child as stupid, the child will come to see herself as stupid; if parents see a child as lazy, then he will develop a self-image as someone who is lazy. Try *Mind, Self and Society* (1934). It's difficult reading (Mead's students compiled this work from their notes) but completely worthwhile. To see what labeling can do to students' performance, read the modern classic by Robert Rosenthal and Lenore Jacobson, *Pygmalion in the Classroom* (1968). Rosenthal and Jacobson told teachers that certain of their students were "bloomers" based on their high IQs. Actually, the so-called bloomers had been chosen at random, and their IQs were no higher than those of students not labeled as bloomers—at least at the beginning of the study. By the end of the year, however, the IQ scores of bloomers were significantly higher than they had been when they entered the class. Apparently, the expectation given to teachers ("These students are superior") was enough to make the labeled children perform at a higher level.

For an excellent summary of research relating self-esteem to chronic social problems, such as child abuse, educational failure, alcohol and drug abuse, welfare dependency, and violent crime, read *The Social Importance of Self-Esteem* (1989), edited by Andrew Mecca, Neil Smelser, and John Vasconcellos. You might be surprised to discover just how much self-image contributes to the really big problems of our day. At the same time, poor self-esteem itself does not develop in a social vacuum; instead, it often develops out of our most difficult social problems, including job displacement, abuse, and educational failure. The relationship between self-esteem and social problems therefore represents a vicious cycle that becomes difficult to break. Where do you intervene? In *Resocialization: An American Experiment* (1973), Daniel Kennedy and August Kerber describe their efforts at *resocializing* individuals who "don't fit in." Such resocialization programs—compensatory education, criminal rehabilitation, and training for the hard-core unemployed—all assume that it is possible to intervene to alter an individual's attitudes, values, and abilities.

For a student-oriented collection of readings about the production and constructions of reality, see Peter Kollock and Jodi O'Brien's *The Production of Reality* (1994). Concerning the effect of television on "Mapping Social Geography," see George Gerbner, Larry Gross, Michael Morgan, and Nancy Signorielli, "Charting the Mainstream: Television's Contributions to Political Orientations," in the *Journal of Communication* (1982). Charles R. Wright, in *Mass Communication: A Sociological Perspective* (1986), discusses the manner in which television cultivates a distorted view of reality. To see the kinds of images being projected for children, read F. Earle Barcus's excellent work, *Images of Life on Children's Television: Sex Roles, Minorities, and Families* (1983). Among other things, Barcus discovered that of the 1,145 characters appearing on children's television, only 42 were black and 47 belonged to some other minority group.

Concerning "Confessions of a Soap Opera Addict," there is plenty of data about the daytime serials in *The Soap Opera* (1983) by Muriel Cantor and Susanne Pingree. For a more general treatment of socialization and mass communication, there are many excellent articles in Sandra Ball-Rokeach and Muriel Cantor's *Media, Audience, and Social Structure* (1986).

Concerning "Foul Play in the Stands," I summarized the experiment conducted by Robert Arms and his colleagues in "Effects of Viewing Aggressive Sports on the Hostility of Spectators," in *Social Psychology Quarterly* (1979). I also cited David Phillips' interesting study, "The Impact of Mass Media Violence on U.S. Homicides," in *American Sociological Review* (1983).

Jeffrey Goldstein's *Aggression and Crimes of Violence* (1986) provides an expanded discussion of the catharsis argument. Like so many others who study the phenomenon, he emphasizes that aggression is often learned by observing others who are rewarded for their aggressive actions.

To understand more about the factors in adulthood that contribute to criminality, read Robert Sampson and John Laub's insightful study, *Crime in the Making: Pathways and Turning Points Through Life* (1994). Sociologists interested in how people are influenced during adulthood have paid a good deal of attention to career socialization—how individuals come to adapt the practices and values of their work experiences. In a classic study, Howard Becker and his colleagues attended medical school classes with regular students to observe the lessons that aspiring physicians were being taught as part of their medical training. The researchers determined that the idealistic and humanitarian views of first-year medical students gradually faded and were replaced by a more practical view of medical knowledge and practice. See *Boys in White* (1961), by Howard S. Becker, Blanche Geer, Everett C. Hughes, and Amselm L. Strauss. More recently, Robert Granfield attended classes at a prestigious Northeastern law school to determine how law students were being socialized to their careers as attorneys. Not unlike what Becker and his associates had discovered concerning medical students, Granfield found that many law students abandoned their idealism in favor of a more cynical form of "thinking like a lawyer." Granfield published his results in "Legal Education as Corporate Ideology," in *Sociological Forum* (1986).

■ DEVELOPING IDEAS *About Socialization*

1. Research topic: Test your own knowledge of social geography. In writing, estimate the percentage of students at your college (or your city)—from 0% to 100%—who are from foreign countries; who are African American, Asian American, and Latin American; and who are women. Now, find a source that can give you an accurate count—the library, the registrar's office, city hall, and so on. How close were your estimates to the actual percentages?

2. Research topic: Communication researchers suggest that television is fixated on appealing to young and wealthy American men, those who buy sponsors' products. As a result, commer-

cial TV does not portray the elderly, minorities, and women as they really are. In fact, many of these groups are virtually absent from the tube.

Analyze one episode of any prime-time dramatic series. In writing, identify the race, ethnic identity, gender, and approximate age (child, teenager, young adult, middle-aged, or old) of each major character. If possible, also find each major character's occupation and social class (from their job, house, car, and so on). If an alien from Mars knew nothing about American society except for what she learned from this one episode, what would she likely conclude about the makeup of the United States?

3. Research topic: Most sociologists believe that the self arises out of social interaction. Cooley's looking-glass self includes this idea. To apply this notion on a personal level, try the following "experiment" suggested by Manford Kuhn's measure of self-concept, his Twenty-Statements Test. Ask a friend to answer, on paper, the question, "Who am I?" with 20 different responses. In analyzing your friend's answers, consider how many relate the self to other people: group memberships (fraternity member, sister, son, and so on) or categories (Catholic, Protestant, American, female, and so on). Kuhn says that children tend to define themselves in very specific terms. For example, they might say they are "nice to a sister" or "good at playing cards." Adults tend to define themselves in much more abstract terms—groups or categories of human beings. If you want to learn more about Kuhn's Twenty-Statements Test, see his 1960 article "Self-Attitudes by Age, Sex, and Professional Training."

4. Writing topic: There is a good deal of evidence that socialization continues throughout life. Robert Granfield and Howard Becker both suggest that students become less idealistic as they are trained formally for a career either in law or medicine. Thinking about these studies as they might apply to your own behavior and attitudes, write an essay in which you play the role of participant-observer to discuss how your personal values and aspirations might have changed as a result of your classroom experiences. Since you first began taking courses at the college level, have you become more or less idealistic in terms of your career objectives? If you have changed, exactly

what do you believe to be responsible for that change? Does your major have something to do with it? Do you ever feel that your instructors are giving you a subtle, perhaps implicit, message about what is important and what is not important in a career, in life? What have you learned from your classmates in this regard?

PART THREE

The Group Experience

I 've lived in the same house since 1976, and I don't even know my next-door neighbor. It's not that I can't remember his name (though I can't). It's that I don't even know what he looks like. Well, I *didn't* know, until the other day. I was standing alone in a train station in Boston, when a complete stranger walked up to me and said, "Aren't you Jack Levin?"

I, of course, nodded my head and asked him politely how he knew me. He told me his name and then informed me that he was my next door neighbor. When I asked him how long he had lived next door, he responded, "For 5 years." Shocked and embarrassed, I welcomed him to the neighborhood. Well, what else was I to do?

The amazing thing is that I live in a middle-class suburb—not in a city apartment, but in a single-family house on a quiet residential street with other single-family houses. Another amazing thing is that I really like people—including my neighbors. But most of my friends and group memberships are somehow associated either with my job or with my family. There seems to be very little room left over in my everyday interaction for the people on my block.

And, then, there is the assumption—perhaps unwarranted—that most of my neighbors are not any different than I am. They have their own lives, too—they are away during the day, probably belong to various organizations at work, probably have a circle of friends and family with whom they share their leisure hours. What kind of an effort have *they* made to get to know me, I ask? (Boy, am I defensive!)

This section is about the experience of being in groups, ranging from families, roommates, neighbors, and peers, on the informal side of the continuum, to the largest organizations—companies, universities, government agencies—you might possibly envision, on the more formal side. *A group provides the social context for interaction between people*—two or more individuals who are aware of one another's presence and who adjust their behavior toward one another. They may talk, laugh, cry, work, play, scream, fight, debate, struggle, or cooperate—but, always, together. This *interaction* is the essence of the group experience. It is also the essence of what sociologists study.

Every member of a group is expected to behave in a certain way, depending on the social position he or she occupies at any given time. Known as a *role*, this bundle of expected behaviors varies—

from giving lectures and grading exams, if you are a teacher, to conversing informally and being supportive, if you are a friend. In the role of physician, an individual is expected to give physical exams and treat illnesses, whereas in the role of homemaker, an individual is expected to feed children and provide shelter. Dentists can stick their fingers in your mouth—but only during working hours. Shoe salesmen can measure your foot size, unless they happen to be in church. And judges can order you in contempt of court, except when they are eating in a restaurant or mowing the lawn at home. In truth, everybody plays a number of different roles every day. The same person who is a dentist may also be a parent, someone's child, a member of the PTA at school, a part-time student at night, a member of a religious congregation, a vice president of a professional organization, a patient, a customer in stores and restaurants, a good friend, a brother or sister, a spouse, and so on. Each and every role played has its own set of expected behaviors—and, typically, we play large numbers of roles every day.

In "Just How Powerful Is a Role?" we learn that many people will go to great lengths—acting in uncharacteristic and bizarre ways—simply to behave in the socially expected manner. The experiment described in this essay suggests that roles can be very powerful in terms of determining how we behave and may also help us understand how atrocities are sometimes committed by normal, even healthy and stable, individuals.

In our mass society, there are people who have little more than superficial contacts with other human beings. Some have no informal contacts at all. Fortunately, while the old, traditional forms of social interaction represented by family and neighborhood may have weakened, they have been replaced by new patterns of interaction. As suggested in "College Fraternities—A Counteracting Force on Campus," students may depend a good deal on fraternities and sororities to find others to date and to develop lasting friendships.

In fact, some people need an excuse just to gather together with others. In "Reunion, American Style," we discover Robert Merton's term *latent function*. He recognized that many of our social arrangements have not only a formal purpose but also an unintended and unrecognized consequence. Professional conferences, for example, frequently held on an annual basis, provide an opportunity for practitioners to exchange information in formal sessions. But the latent and therefore unintended, unrecognized effect may be even more important. In bars, restaurants, and hotel lobbies, participants from around the country reunite to "chat." Their informal conversations often provide the basis for exchanging ideas and collaborating on projects. In the same article, we see the manner in which patterns of behavior can become *institutionalized*. That is, aspects of the social order become widely accepted and organized. In our society, class reunions have become big business, a commercial success.

Speaking of big business and big organizations, "Children of the Organization Men" takes a look at two generations: first, those men (there were very few women who did this) who came of age in the 1950s and worked for most of their careers in large organizations. What happened to their children? Did they become organization men and women? Or did they choose to follow a different career path for themselves? A recent study of "organizational offspring" indicates that their fathers' loyalty to corporations and conformity to social order were hardly passed on to the next generation. Instead, the sons and daughters of organization men turned their attention to the self and cherished raw individualism. ∎

Just How Powerful Is a Role?
Ask the Prisoners and Guards on Campus

Is it possible for people who are ordinarily decent, caring, and kind to behave as though they are sadistic and cruel—just because we expect them to be? Can the structure of social situations make normal people do crazy, sickening, immoral things?

At the Nuremberg trials for "crimes against humanity" perpetrated in the concentration camps during World War II, Nazi leaders typically looked so normal, so ordinary, so much like the rest of us. Yet they were eventually found guilty of organizing and carrying out mass executions. In addition, thousands of German citizens went along and obeyed orders, even if it meant committing atrocities.

An important study by Philip Zimbardo and his associates at Stanford University may help shed light on the phenomenon of normal people doing abnormal, even horrific, things to others. Zimbardo and his colleagues turned the basement of a building on campus into a mock prison. They created a number of "cells" by installing bars and locks on each room and then placing a cot in each one.

Twenty student volunteers—all chosen for their mature and stable personalities—were selected to participate in the study. On a purely random basis (i.e., the flip of a coin), half of the students were assigned to play the role of guards, and the other half were assigned to play the role of prisoners.

The experiment actually started at the homes of the 10 student "prisoners." To increase the realism of the study, all of them were "arrested," put in handcuffs, read their rights, and then driven to "jail" in police cars. They were then completely stripped, sprayed with disinfectants, issued prison uniforms, and placed into locked cells.

Everyone knew that the experiment was artificial and that it was supposed to end in 2 weeks. Nobody was *really* a prisoner; nobody was *really* a guard. It was pure make-believe, having been decided by the flip of a coin. Yet after only a few days, both the prisoners and the guards were playing their roles with frightening determination. Guards were told only to keep order. Instead, they began to humiliate and embarrass the prisoners, coercing them to remain silent on command, to sing or laugh in front of the other inmates, and to clean up messes made by the guards. In some cases, the guards would verbally and physically threaten and intimidate the prisoners— apparently for the purpose of asserting their authority.

For their part, the prisoners became more and more passive and compliant. In accord with the roles to which they had been assigned, the prisoners obeyed orders and accepted commands, no matter how unreasonable. They began to feel totally powerless to fight back. After only 6 days, four of the prisoners had to be excused from the study, having suffered serious episodes of anxiety, anger, or depression. In fact, the entire experiment was ended in less than 1 week when it became clear that the guards had become abusive and the prisoners were emotionally at risk.

Interviews conducted after the experiment ended were revealing. Both the "prisoners" and the "guards" told Zimbardo and his associates that they were both shocked and ashamed at how they had behaved. None of them would have predicted that they were capable of such cruelty, in the case of the guards, or obedience to authority, in the case of the prisoners. Remember that all of the student volunteers had been selected for their mature and stable personalities. Yet they all acted according to the roles created by the structure of prison life.

How powerful is a role? Just ask the students who volunteered to participate in Zimbardo's study. Then think of the atrocities committed in Nazi Germany! ▪

College Fraternities—A Counteracting Force on Campus

Where Else Would Students Get to Know One Another?

Those who long for a return to a time of strong family ties, neighborliness, and a simpler life often invoke the term *mass society* to characterize a long-standing trend in American society that they deplore. The image of mass society is all too familiar to millions of Americans in the 1990s—people who feel very much alone, city dwellers and suburbanites living in "boxes," dissatisfied customers who talk on the phone to automated voices, rush-hour traffic that won't quit, and waiting lines a mile long.

All of these forms of mass society are, indeed, a painful fact of life for millions of Americans. Yet at the same time that older types of social relations have diminished, they have been replaced by new, and sometimes deceptively effective, forms of intimacy and informality that compensate for the loss of traditional primary ties and counteract feelings of loneliness and isolation.

Technology has provided some degree of compensation. Even when friends and relatives are physically separated, they can still sustain primary contacts by telephone. Or as a postmodern form of social interaction, they can keep in touch by means of personal computer (Internet, E-mail, and electronic bulletin boards), even if they are thousands of miles apart.

Of course, technological devices such as long-distance telephones and computers hardly make up for the eclipse of community in America. Their essentially superficial forms of interaction cannot possibly compensate totally for the loss of profound friendship and family networks found in the neighborhoods or communities of another era.

This can be seen clearly in the case of millions of college students around the country who leave their families—perhaps for the first time ever—to take up residence on a campus, sometimes located thousands of miles from home. It should come as no surprise that these students, especially if they are on large and diverse campuses, often search for opportunities for intimacy and friendship. Some find the primary contacts they need in fraternities and sororities.

Membership in college fraternities and sororities seems to ebb and flow, depending on the social circumstances surrounding campus life at a particular point in time. In 1966, some 30% of all college students belonged to Greek-letter societies; by 1976, however, this figure had dropped to only 19% nationally. In fact, fully two thirds of these colleges had experienced declining fraternity enrollments. During the 1970s, on some campuses across the country, fraternities completely disappeared.

Apparently, the fraternity's ability to counteract mass society on campus was overruled, at least during this period of time, by a more powerful theme among the college-bound baby boomer generation. Many college students of the early 1970s regarded fraternity membership as thoroughly inconsistent with their interests in civil rights, student rights, antiwar activism, feminism, racial equality, and independence from institutional constraints.

James A. Fox and I conducted a study showing that the disappearance of college fraternities was short-lived. By examining the fraternity and sorority membership figures around the country, we discovered a major resurgence of interest in campus fraternities. By 1981, almost one half of all colleges and universities had already reported seeing growth in fraternity enrollments. As more and more students sought structured opportunities to meet other students, date, and develop friendships, the fraternity began to make its big comeback. Especially on campuses where most of the students came from outside of the immediate area, there were few commuters, and there was little else to attract students in the wider community, fraternity membership thrived and prospered. In some southern schools, fraternity membership reached 80%.

In a mass society, independence can be very lonely. For college students who miss the intimacy of family life, fraternities and sororities provide a new set of "brothers" and "sisters"—and a home away from home. ■

Reunion, American Style
The Ritual of Recommuning

In her novel of the same name, Rona Jaffe suggests that a class reunion "is more than a sentimental journey. It is also a way of answering the question that lies at the back of nearly all our minds. Did they do better than I?"

Jaffe's observation may be misplaced but not completely lost. According to a study conducted by social psychologist Jack Sparacino, the overwhelming majority who attend reunions aren't there invidiously to compare their recent accomplishments with those of their former classmates. Instead, they hope, primarily, to relive their earlier successes.

Certainly, a few return to show their former classmates how well they have done; others enjoy observing the changes that have occurred in their classmates (but not always in themselves, of course). But the majority who attend their class reunions do so to relive the good times they remember having when they were younger. In his study, Sparacino found that, as high school students, attendees had been more popular, more often regarded as attractive, and more involved in extracurricular activities than those classmates who chose not to attend. For those who turned up at their reunions, then, the old times were also the good times!

It would appear that Americans have a special fondness for reunions, judging by their prevalence. Major league baseball players, fraternity members, veterans groups, high school and college graduates, and former Boy Scouts all hold reunions on a regular basis. In addition, family reunions frequently attract blood relatives from faraway places who spend considerable money and time to reunite.

Actually, in their affection for reuniting with friends, family, or colleagues, Americans are probably no different from any other people, except that Americans have created a mind-boggling number and variety of *institutionalized* forms of gatherings to facilitate the satisfaction of this desire. Indeed, reunions have increasingly become formal events that are organized on a regular basis and, in the process, they have also become *big business*.

Shell Norris of Class Reunion, Inc., says that Chicago alone has 1,500 high school reunions each year. A conservative estimate on the national level would be 10,000 annually. At one time, all high school reunions were organized by volunteers, usually female homemakers. In the last few years, however, as more and more women have entered the labor force, alumni reunions are increasingly being planned by specialized companies rather than by part-time volunteers.

The first college reunion was held by the alumni of Yale University in 1792. Graduates of Pennsylvania, Princeton, Stanford, and Brown followed suit. And by the end of the 19th century, most 4-year institutions were holding alumni reunions.

According to Paul Chewning, vice president for alumni administration at the Council for Advancement and Support of Education (CASE), the variety of college reunions is impressive. At Princeton, alumni parade through the town wearing their class uniforms and singing their alma mater. At Marietta College, they gather for a dinner-dance on a steamship cruising the Ohio River. At Dartmouth, alumni act as lecturers and panelists in continuing education courses for their former classmates.

Clearly, the thought of cruising on a steamship or marching through the streets is usually not, by itself, sufficient reason for large numbers of alumni to return to campus. Chewning contends that alumni who decide to attend their reunions share a common identity based on the years they spent together as undergraduates. For this reason, universities that somehow establish a common bond—for example, because they are relatively small or especially prestigious—tend to draw substantial numbers of their alumni to reunions. In an effort to enhance this common identity, larger colleges and universities frequently build their class reunions on participation in smaller units, such as departments or schools. Or they encourage "affinity reunions" for groups of former cheerleaders, editors, fraternity members, musicians, members of military organizations on campus, and the like.

Of course, not every alumnus is fond of his or her alma mater. Michelle Favreault, Associate Director of Alumni Affairs at Brandeis University, suggests that students who graduated during the late 1960s may be especially reluctant to get involved in alumni events. They were part of the generation that conducted sit-ins and teach-ins directed at university administrators, protested Reserve Officers' Training Corps (ROTC) and military recruitment on campus, and marched against "establishment politics." If this generation has a common identity, it may fall outside of their university ties—or even be hostile to them. Even as they enter their middle years, alumni who continue to hold unpleasant memories of college during this period may not wish to attend class reunions.

Not all reunions are school affairs. People also reunite as an unintended consequence, a latent function of gatherings designed for other reasons. Hundreds of professional associations hold annual conferences or conventions to keep their members up-to-date with developments in their fields. Yet many of the professionals who attend pass up the formal sessions—the speeches and seminars—in favor of meeting informally in bars and hotel lobbies with colleagues from other cities and states. Attendees are given an excuse to swap experiences with friends they haven't seen since the last meeting. Similarly, the manifest function—the intended and recognized purpose—of wedding ceremonies is to unite the bride and groom in matrimony. Yet weddings (as well as funerals, confirmations, and bar mitzvahs) also serve an important latent function: They provide occasions for scattered families and friends to reunite.

The poignancy of these meetings suggests a more general principle: If reunions make people cry, it is not, as Rona Jaffe proposes, because they have come out on the short end of things *now*. It is because they measured up so well 20 years ago, and they want to relive the good old days with tears of joy. ∎

Children of the Organization Men
The New Individualists

For more than 30 years, William H. Whyte's *The Organization Man* was the most widely read book about organizational life. Focusing on middle-class Americans at midcentury, Whyte argued that bureaucratic organizations actually shaped almost every aspect of our lives. They dictated that employees be "groupminded." That is, they were expected to be flexible to the demands of others, to be completely loyal to the corporation, and to remain uncommitted to a set of values. In this view, organizations rewarded only those individuals who were "good team players." Nothing else really counted, from the corporate point of view.

In collecting data for his book, Whyte followed his organization men (this is not a sexist slight; there simply weren't any organization women) into their offices, but he also visited their suburban homes, schools, and neighborhoods. He interviewed their wives and observed their children.

Whyte's description of the social role of the corporate wife is particularly telling. Any employee who aspired to be promoted to an executive position needed a wife who obeyed the corporate rules. She had to be willing to make frequent moves from city to city for the sake of her husband's job, to assume exclusive responsibility for household chores and child rearing, and to stay away from her husband's workplace. She must never gossip about the office with other corporate wives, never get drunk at a company party, never be too friendly with the wives of other employees whom her husband might pass on his way up the corporate ladder, and never show up her husband by being superior to him in any way.

Whyte observed the rise of a pervasive *social ethic*—a widely held belief that the group was the essential source of creativity and that "belongingness" was *the* basic human need. Thus, the demand for "yes-men," "happy homemakers," "family togetherness," and "team players." Hence, the worship of the organization.

For their book, *The New Individualists: The Generation After the Organization Man*, Paul Leinberger (whose father was an organization man interviewed 30 years earlier by William Whyte) and Bruce Tucker recently interviewed the sons and daughters of the original organization men as well as hundreds of other "organizational off-spring." They focused on baby boomer Americans—those men and women born between 1946 and 1964 whose fathers had worked for most of their careers in large organizations. Included in their study were "the middle manager chafing at the slow progress up the promotional ladder, the forest ranger dreaming of writing novels, the aging hippie getting by on marginal jobs, the gypsy scholar in to-day's brutal academic job market, the entrepreneur starting a soft-ware company, the corporate star rising rapidly, and the free-lance consultant seeking autonomy."

Leinberger and Tucker found that the organizational offspring were very different from their fathers in terms of outlook, values, and motives. Children of organization men resembled one another with respect to attitude toward organizations, style of interpersonal rela-tions, and patterns of consumption. But unlike their fathers, all of them were strong individualists. Whereas organization men admired the salesman, their offspring admire the artist. Whereas organization men were conspicuous consumers, their children cherish creativity. Whereas organization men were dominated by sociability, their off-spring pursue self-fulfillment.

Leinberger and Tucker suggest that social change is partially re-sponsible for the new norms embraced by organizational offspring. During the past 30 years, we have seen major changes in the condi-tions of work, leisure, economics, family life, and politics. The huge number of acquisitions and mergers in the late 1980s makes a lie of the concept of corporate loyalty; many longtime executives were summarily dismissed without any cause other than a need to reduce corporate expenses. The dual-career family introduces competing sources of allegiance between work and home. Foreign competition and reduced profits put new strains on American business.

The resulting generational differences are often profound. As soon as they finished school, organization men married, went to work, and began having children. By their mid-30s, the last of their 2 or 3 children was born. By contrast, children of the organization men often remain in school through their 20s, marry even later, and are in their 30s when they have their 1.8 children.

An obsession with the self can be observed as a major element in the individualism of the organizational offspring. At home, in schools, and through the mass media, the members of this genera-tion were urged to enhance "self-expression," "self-fulfillment," "self-actualization," "self-assertion," "self-understanding," and "self-acceptance." Just as surely as their parents accepted a social ethic, the children of the organization men developed a *self ethic*.

The organization men were severely criticized for their almost robotlike obedience to corporate aspirations. But their children's individualistic ideal has also come under attack. According to Leinberger and Tucker, the offspring have created the most radical version of the individual in American history—a thoroughly isolated individual who can't make commitments, can't communicate, can't achieve community. The exclusive emphasis on the self has left many people feeling alone and anxious.

To the extent that organizational offspring remain committed to the self ethic, they are unlikely to provide the human resources for a competitive American work force—not unless the corporation adjusts to them. This is no small problem. There are approximately 19 million adult children of the organization men. What is more, as the offspring of the managerial class, they represent the middle and upper-middle classes—the very people who have historically dominated American business.

The management philosophy of the organization man generation survives. Into the 1990s, corporate managers continue to revere professionalism, control, teamwork, and order. At the same time, they have little patience with the ideas of leadership, substance, or vision. At midcentury, when American companies had no real competition, the organization man's view of corporate reality was viable enough. In the contemporary world of global competition and economic uncertainty, however, vision and leadership may be essential for survival. In the long haul, quality becomes more important than quantity.

Leinberger and Tucker present the grounds for believing that for children of the organization men, the future holds a better fit between their personal style and structural demands. If they are to succeed in the long run, organizations will be required to adapt themselves to a new generation of individualists—men and women who will soon be replacing their fathers in leadership positions. But just in case they don't adapt, perhaps it is time that we study the next generation—the grandchildren of the organization men. ∎

■ **FOCUS** *Suggestions for Further Reading*

The classic prison role experiment conducted by Philip Zimbardo and his colleagues Craig Haney and William Banks is described in detail in "A Pirandellian Prison" in the *New York Times Magazine* (1973). For a famous study of obedient role-playing, also read Stanley Milgram's *Obedience to Authority: An Experimental View* (1974). In Milgram's study, 60% of a sample of normal Americans were willing to administer a severe electrical shock to a stranger, simply because they were told to do so by an authority figure in a lab coat.

Concerning "College Fraternities—A Counteracting Force on Campus," the original idea of counteracting forces in mass society can be found in Arnold Rose's article, "Reactions Against the Mass Society," in the *Sociological Quarterly* (1962.) For a recent treatment of the individual in modern, postmodern, or hypermodern society (depending on your personal view), read the fascinating account by George Ritzer in *The McDonaldization of Society* (1993).

I collected information for "Reunion, American Style" by interviewing alumni personnel in a number of colleges and universities. I also relied on data gathered by the Alumni Administration Division of the Council for the Advancement and Support of Education (CASE). If you are interested in learning more about class reunions, I suggest getting in touch with CASE in Washington, D.C. Concerning the functional argument used in this snapshot, Robert K. Merton's *Social Theory and Social Structure* (1957) is an important work in which he discusses, among many other things, the distinction between manifest and latent functions. He also discusses the role of serendipity in science, a topic that will be raised later in this book when we consider social change.

Concerning "Children of the Organization Men," the classic treatment of the midcentury lifestyle of the loyal and obedient corporate employee can be found in William H. Whyte's *The Organization Man* (1956). Conclusions in this snapshot regarding the children of organization men were drawn from *The New Individualists: The Generation After the Organization Man* (1991), by Paul Leinberger and Bruce Tucker. For an enlightening account of how bureaucratic organizations systematically hinder the careers of women, read Rosabeth M. Kanter's *Men and Women of the Corporation* (1993).

■ DEVELOPING IDEAS *About the Group Experience*

1. Research topic: One of the most fundamental forms of social order is contained in the concept of *role,* the set of expected behaviors associated with a particular social position, such as teacher, doctor, son, mother, student, and so on. What is OK in one role may be totally inappropriate in another. For example, we expect students to take exams, write papers, and attend class. We do not expect them to stick their fingers in someone's mouth. But dentists do it every day (we actually pay dentists to stick their fingers in our mouths), and we don't expect dentists to write papers. What is proper or improper depends on the role.

   As you know, there is even a role of elevator rider. Similarly, there is a role of passenger, whether on a bus, train, or airplane. While riding with strangers on public transportation, we are expected to behave in a certain way. To examine the requirements of this role, take a ride on a bus or other form of public transportation (if this is too difficult, try riding in an elevator). While acting as a passenger, notice how other riders are sitting or standing, whether there is any conversation (if so, about what and under what circumstances?), and how you feel when the vehicle is crowded and why you feel that way. If you are not too embarrassed to do so, you might try starting a conversation with another passenger. What is the reaction?

2. Research topic: Do college organizations really compensate for a lack of informal interaction? If so, students who spend much time with family, partners, or friends shouldn't join many clubs and organizations on campus; students who don't hang out with family, partners, or friends should make up the difference by joining. Interview a number of students on your campus to find out as much as you can about their social activities: how often they are with friends or family, how many campus organizations they belong to, any leadership positions they hold in these organizations. What do your results indicate about college organizations as compensatory groups?

3. Writing topic: Examine an institutionalized practice—for example, a wedding or a funeral—for all of the *latent* functions it might perform.

4. Research topic: Just how restrictive is a formal organization? To what extent does holding a job in a large corporation necessitate a loss of personal freedom for the individual who works there? To provide a case study, visit a large company in your local community. For at least a few hours, observe the patterns of behavior—including dress, speech, arrangement of furniture in offices, any uniformity of color, hairstyles, cars in the parking lot, schedule for lunch and breaks, and so on. Don't forget to take notes concerning your observations in some systematic way. For example, before beginning, you might want to make a partial list of the patterns of behavior you expect to find, to be expanded during the study. You might even want to visit, only briefly, another large company, to get ideas about how employees conform. By the way, to avoid looking suspicious while collecting data, you might want to inform someone at the company of your purpose and ask permission to become a participant-observer.

PART FOUR

Institutions

A t a time when today's aging baby boomers were still hippies—during the late 1960s and early 1970s—I was just finishing up my graduate degree and making plans for the future. My primary objective was to teach at the college level. Yet not unlike many of my friends and fellow graduate students in sociology, I also thought long and hard about the possibility of dropping out of the mainstream of competitive American society and establishing instead an alternative lifestyle that would be less demanding and repressive. In retrospect, it sounds kind of silly; but at the time, it seemed to make sense.

During the late 1960s, many young people claimed to have given up on American institutions—the nuclear family, organized religion, capitalism, constitutional government, and traditional forms of public education—and it was relatively easy to find support and encouragement for going it alone. The more politically motivated students of the day referred to anyone in charge of almost anything—whether the police, the chair of the sociology department, or the president of the United States—as "pigs" and to conventional, middle-class political institutions, in the most negative sense possible, as "the establishment." Even among students who weren't inclined toward politics, the operating principle of everyday life seemed to be "do your own thing." Traditional institutions—the traditional ways of meeting basic needs—were often viewed as irrelevant, if not the enemy.

Of course, though many hip-oriented students paid lip service to the idea of an alternative lifestyle, most never went much beyond the hippie fashion (wearing love beads, jeans, and long hair) in seeking to throw off what they saw as the yoke of repression represented by American institutions. Even the antiwar demonstrations and demonstrations for civil rights and women were, for the most part, designed to reform, not overthrow, traditional institutional arrangements. After all, many of those young people who demonstrated loudly for equal rights or against the war were students enrolled in the very colleges and universities they were fiercely attacking. Moreover, only a relatively few young people actually left school to drop out of American society.

Over time, those who did leave to take up residence on a commune attempted to establish their own institutions—frequently, collective arrangements for feeding their families, building shelter, making clothing, teaching the basic skills of everyday life to children, and attending to their spiritual needs. Many communes failed to survive for more than a few months, however, because they also failed to develop collective ways for meeting their members' basic needs. In a word, they never developed viable alternative institutions.

The collective ways developed by any society for meeting the economic, religious, familial, political, and educational needs of its members are known as *institutions*. The lesson to be learned from the failure of many hippie communes of the 1960s and 1970s is simply that a group of people cannot survive very long as a group without generating some set of effective institutional arrangements. The more recent demise of the Soviet Union was, in part, a result of a profound failure of its institutions in terms of meeting the basic needs of its members. It can happen to a small commune or to an entire society of millions of people.

How well do American institutions meet human needs? In "Who's Minding the Kids?" we find a very negative answer: our families, schools, and religious institutions are so weak that the adolescent peer group has taken over. Young people now raise one another. As a result, violence among teenagers has taken on epidemic proportions.

Institutions often provide an efficiency in meeting human needs that would be impossible by sheer individual effort alone. But on the social psychological level, institutional responsiveness to difficult social problems also allows human beings to avoid dealing firsthand with what they desire to pretend doesn't exist—death, illness, disaster, disfigurement, and disability. In "Let the System Do It!" this idea is introduced and illustrated. We have developed a set of institutions—schools, political systems, corporations, legal units, and religions—each of which now carries out specialized functions that used to be performed by family members. As a result, we, as individual members of society, escape the burden of having to face the entire range of human issues and frailties.

The students who attend our institutions of higher education have changed in important ways. They now represent a wider range of differences, and they are organized. Twenty-five years ago, special-interest organizations on campus included fraternities and a few religious groups. Today, however, there are likely to be organized groups for African Americans, gay men and lesbians, Latinos, Asians, women, students with disabilities, and international students, to mention just a few. In "Diversity on Campus," we see that college students aren't always prepared to deal with their schoolmates who are different with respect to race, religion, sexual orientation, disability status, or even gender.

One of the most important functions of the economic institution involves getting the unpleasant but necessary jobs done. In "Dirty Work," we are reminded that dirty work in America has traditionally been performed at low wages by poor people, newcomers, and minorities who have had few other choices. We also see that the "dirtiness" of a job has little, if anything, to do with its being physically unclean but can be changed profoundly depending on how much we pay people to do it. ∎

Who's Minding the Kids?

Is Violence Filling the Void in Our Teenagers' Lives?

Daily, the headlines scream of hideous crimes—drive-by shootings, carjackings, and senseless murders—committed by our nation's teenagers. What makes violence so appealing to so many youngsters? Why is it that, in many quarters around the country, guns have replaced leather jackets and CD players as status symbols of choice?

According to police reports to the FBI, the number of homicides committed by youngsters in their early teens has recently skyrocketed. Between 1985 and 1991, arrest rates for homicide increased among 13- and 14-year-old males by 140%; among 15-year-old males by 217%.

Actually, the problem is even worse than these dreadful statistics might suggest. While relatively few of our youngsters are committing hideous murders, they are being tolerated—perhaps even honored—by their friends and classmates. Millions of teenagers may not be able to shoot or stab someone themselves, but they are fully capable of looking on as others do so.

Several years ago, a case of bystander apathy raised enough concern to inspire the movie *River's Edge*. A teenager in Milpitas, California, murdered his 14-year-old girlfriend and then returned to the scene with a dozen classmates to show them the corpse. One student covered the body with leaves to keep it from being discovered; others threw rocks at it. None of them contacted the police or told their parents.

More recently, the nation was shocked to learn that an attractive New Hampshire school teacher, Pam Smart, had inspired her 15-year-old student and his friends to eliminate her husband, Greg, by shooting him in the head. Attorney Marsha Kazarosian subsequently filed a suit against the Winnecunnet, New Hampshire, school district on behalf of the families of the three youngsters convicted in the murder. Kazarosian claimed that Pam Smart's love affair with her student was made possible because she was negligently unsupervised by the Winnecunnet High School administration—that somebody in charge should have been keeping a watchful eye on Smart.

Whether or not school officials should have known, it appears that they may have been the only ones at Winnecunnet High who didn't.

Statements made during the course of the police investigation indicate clearly that at least 1 month before the police finally broke the case, the corridors of Winnecunnet High were already abuzz with rumors implicating the three students and their teacher. Yet nobody bothered to inform an adult.

More incredibly, statements later made to law enforcement officials indicate that students at Winnecunnet High were talking about Greg Smart's murder for 2 months *before* it actually occurred. With a simple phone call, any one of them might have prevented a murder. But nobody wanted to "snitch" or "tattle" on a classmate. Everybody was concerned about being rejected by friends. So they all kept quiet and let the murder plot proceed according to plan.

Too many of our teenagers have become desensitized to the consequences of violence. They have been raised on a steady diet of slasher films filled with gory scenes of sex, murder, and mayhem. After school, they come home to an empty house, where they spend hours daily listening to rap and heavy metal lyrics or watching MTV videos in which violence is glorified. For economic reasons, more and more of our teenagers are left to fend for themselves, unsupervised after school and during vacations.

Only a few of our youngsters are willing to shoot someone in the head. But many others participate from a distance. Even if breaking their silence might stop a murder, they do not want to get involved.

It may have happened in New Hampshire, but it could have been anywhere. Marsha Kazarosian's lawsuit reflects an unpleasant truth about American society today. It isn't that TV, motion pictures, and popular music are so powerful. It is that our traditional institutions have become so weak. Our schools, religions, and families have lost their moral authority. And in their place, we have allowed the peer group to fill the void in our youngsters' lives. ∎

Let the System Do It!
Taking Care of Society's Problems Can Hurt

Less than a century ago, the middle-class family was still involved in almost every aspect of its members' lives. Mother, father, grand-parents, and children all worked the farm (or in the family firm). Together, they educated the offspring, treated illnesses, and provided a role for elders. After death, family members were buried in the family plot in the backyard, not in some cemetery with thousands of strangers located miles away.

In responding to social problems, we have similarly constructed hospitals, prisons, nursing homes, and "special" schools for the re-tarded and the emotionally disturbed. In the same way, we have built mental institutions, cancer wards, soup kitchens, and retirement communities—all in the name of efficiency and humanitarian moti-vation.

Clearly, there are compelling administrative, medical, and eco-nomic reasons why many of our thorniest human problems—illness, poverty, and old age—are better handled by specialized formal orga-nizations than by families. But there may be other, less rational, reasons as well.

One clue is to look at the sites where our nation's prisons and mental hospitals were first located. Many of them are now in mid-dle-class suburban areas, an easy drive from the urban core. But at the time they were built, these same areas were quite different—they were almost invariably secluded rural settings, located many miles from large population centers and hidden from everyday view. Even cemeteries were typically built some distance from major cities, allowing friends and relatives to pay a visit but only on a limited basis.

Remember the cliche, "out of sight, out of mind"? Let's face it: There are many problems that middle-class Americans would prefer to shuttle aside and put out of easy reach. Too often, the attitude is, "Let somebody else take care of it. We aren't trained and they are."

Thus, our formal organizations help us to isolate those things we simply don't want to see. By constructing a formal response, we are able to avoid the whole range of human misery that might otherwise disrupt our personal lives and make us feel very uncomfortable. By letting the formal system take care of terminal cancer patients, drug addicts, severely disfigured individuals, and Alzheimer's victims, for example, we increase the *subjective probability* that these hideous things won't happen to us or to our loved ones. By distancing ourselves from human frailty and misery, we are then free to pursue our individual goals and objectives—at work and at home—without fear that *the same thing might (or will) happen to us.*

Specialized institutions give us the false security of being able to go through life avoiding life's problems—until we are forced to deal with them. This may be one reason why community-based forms of treatment for mental illness, retardation, and juvenile delinquency have so often been opposed by Americans. In too many cases, even where their residents pose little if any risk to the neighbors, the thinking is that halfway houses belong on anybody else's block but mine.

Of course, not everyone opts to put their blinders on. Recognizing the myopic view of many Americans, educators are beginning to stress the importance of exposing young people to the entire range of social problems that they might otherwise not encounter. In one special program for high school students, for example, each teenager in the program spends one day working in a home for retarded children; each spends a number of hours in a jail cell; and each pays a visit to a morgue. They may get sick to their stomachs, but they also learn about the possible consequences of their own behavior as well as the inevitable consequences of being human. They are forced to see the world the way it really is; and not the way they'd like it to be. In the process, they may unexpectedly come face-to-face with themselves. ■

Diversity on Campus
College Students Aren't Immune to Bigotry and Hatred

The National Institute Against Prejudice and Violence in Baltimore reports that college students on campuses aren't necessarily getting along with their diverse classmates, roommates, and schoolmates. Indeed, the institute has discovered a dramatic increase in racial and anti-Semitic incidents on campuses around the country. At more than 160 colleges, there has been at least a single "intergroup" episode during a 3-year period, ranging from acts of insensitivity to episodes of open warfare. The institute estimates that 20% of all minority college students are either physically or verbally harassed. Over a 1-year period, the rise in anti-Semitic incidents alone approached 30%.

Such incidents, usually initiated by college students themselves, have included shattering the windows of a Jewish student center in a burst of gunfire, publishing Hitler's statements in the campus newspaper, assaulting members of a Jewish fraternity, spray painting the words "white power" on the walls of an Afro-American cultural center, airing racist jokes on the campus radio station, harassing a black professor, and scribbling racist graffiti on restroom doors. In a few cases, students have actually been murdered simply because they are different.

The targets of campus hate crimes have encompassed a broad range of students aside from blacks and Jews, including whites, Asians, Latinos, Native Americans, and women. Moreover, spurred by the war in the Persian Gulf, dark-skinned students with foreign accents—especially those coming from middle-eastern nations—were frequently regarded as the "enemy" by American college students looking for someone, perhaps anyone, to blame.

The most persecuted students on college campuses do not, however, necessarily differ from their assailants with respect to race, religion, national origin, or even gender; they differ in terms of sexual orientation. According to many observers, lesbian and gay students have been most frequently targeted for victimization. On college campuses, gay students have been held hostage, verbally harassed with insulting comments, had their books and clothing defaced, and received anonymous death threats. During Gay Pride Week on one campus, a number of men burst into a movie being watched by a gay group on campus and then blocked the exits to the room. On another campus, several students wore sweatshirts bearing the logo "Anti-Fag Society." After a college dance marathon in the Midwest, a gay couple was threatened with death on their answering machine. At an East Coast university, antigay slurs were scrawled on sidewalks on the central campus.

But you don't have to be gay to be victimized—you only have to "look gay." Male students who appear to be effeminate with regard to their body language or speech may be regularly harassed by their peers in college dormitories or campus centers. At the same time, such indicators of sexual orientation can be unreliable; there are effeminate men who aren't gay and gay men who aren't effeminate.

This is a major reason why attacks against gays and lesbians are so often targeted at their campus offices and organizational meetings. Based on appearance alone, haters cannot always identify students who are gay. As a result, they look for places where they are sure to find a number of "them" together. Frequently, the flyers announcing a meeting are torn down or defaced. At one university recently, campus bigots scribbled their message, "All faggots must die," across the announcements. At the same university, an anonymous caller phoned the office of the campus Gay and Lesbian Coalition to say, "I'm a Nazi skinhead. I'm going to bomb your office and blow all you fags up."

Some college students sincerely believe, often on religious grounds, that homosexuality is immoral. It would be difficult, if not impossible, to convince such students otherwise. But even the most homophobic people on campus can usually be dissuaded from attacking gays in a violent or hurtful way. First, however, they must come to see gay students on campus as what they are: human beings. ■

Dirty Work
Who's Going to Do the Unpleasant Jobs?

Every society has its "dirty work": jobs that are considered repugnant, undignified, or menial. They may also be regarded as absolutely essential for the well-being of society. Throughout the world, much of the dirtiest work of a society has been reserved for those individuals considered to be outside the mainstream; for example, Pakistanis in England, Iraquis in Kuwait, and Turks in Germany. At the same time, even the most prestigious occupations may include at least a few tasks that could be regarded as dirty.

As a historical trend, the increasing rationalization of American society has created a proliferation of specialized occupations from what was formerly thought of as merely another field's dirty work. Indeed, millions of Americans currently work in jobs that never even existed a few decades earlier: assistants to activity directors in nursing homes and day care centers, emergency medical technicians, dental hygienists, data entry personnel, paralegals, associate producers, home care workers, audiovisual equipment aides, television and radio interns, and so on. To an increasing extent, therefore, one occupation's dirty work has become another's raison d'être!

In the midst of the expansion of specialized occupational roles, some professionals have gained enough resources to subcontract much, if not all, of their dirty work to lower-paid specialists. For example, professors may assign the task of grading multiple-choice exams to their teaching assistants; many dentists have hygienists who perform routine dental care; and nurses often enlist nurses' aides to change bandages and bedpans. Accountants have their bookkeepers, physicians have physicians' assistants, and lawyers have paralegals.

What comes to be viewed as dirty work need not be the least bit dirty, at least in a physical sense. There is really nothing intrinsically repulsive about what we might choose to call dirty work. Instead, jobs are labeled as respectable or dirty based typically on a social construction: The members of a society share an understanding of the nature of their environment and apply that understanding to their definitions of occupational tasks.

In contemporary American society, for example, bankers are generally seen as holding a reputable occupational position. During the Middle Ages, however, the same job was regarded as too dirty for Christians to perform and was instead assigned to outsiders—specifically, to European Jews who were systematically excluded from respectable activities, such as farming, owning land, and joining the guilds of craftsmen. Generally, Jews were restricted to the despised occupation of lending money at interest—an activity regarded as essential by the church and the nobility as a source of outside financing for building, farming, waging war, or engaging in political affairs.

Its economic importance notwithstanding, usury was absolutely forbidden to the Christian majority on religious grounds. As viewed by the church, the lending of money for interest was sinful regardless of the amount of interest charged or the purpose for which money was borrowed. Thus, any Christian who lent money during the Middle Ages would have committed a mortal sin. In the view of the medieval church, however, Jews were headed for hell anyway, so their participation in money lending could add little to the eternal punishment that already awaited them in the hereafter.

Traditionally, dirty work in America has been performed at low wages by poor people, newcomers, and minorities who have had few other choices. In the southern colonies, slaves were forced to play the role of field hands or domestic servants, and indentured servants performed heavy labor to buy their freedom. During the 19th century, Chinese newcomers toiled to build the railroads and work the crops. At the turn of the 20th century, European immigrants performed unskilled, backbreaking labor for poor wages and under miserable working conditions.

Even today, many economic activities involving dirty work in areas such as restaurants, hospitals, and industrial agriculture continue to rely heavily on people from outside the mainstream—Americans of color and newcomers from Latin America, Asia, and Eastern Europe. According to sociologist Herbert Gans, these activities could not survive in their present form without depending on the substandard wages that they pay to their employees. More generally, Gans suggests that poverty may actually persist in part because it serves the important function of providing a low-wage labor pool that is willing to perform dirty work at low cost.

Of course, many respectable jobs also involve at least some tasks that most people would consider boring and unpleasant, even if they don't require getting their hands dirty. Take, for example, the role of police officer, which, according to the television image, consists exclusively of battling the forces of evil. Actually, the police spend much of their time and energy on more mundane matters, such as removing dead mice, controlling traffic, doing paperwork, helping citizens who have fallen out of bed, and answering false alarms. Many police officers actually go through an entire career without ever having to fire their weapons in the line of duty.

To complicate matters, the very meaning of what comes to be regarded as dirty work is partially determined by the prestige level of an occupation. Indeed, the same tasks may be considered dirty when performed for low wages but respectable and clean when performed for a lot of money. Homemakers who are unpaid for providing services to the members of their family may occasionally feel bored with routine child rearing and the daily drudgery of preparing the evening meal, yet such tasks are not intrinsically boring. In fact, they are quite pleasant and satisfying—when carried out by a well-paid teacher or by a chef in a gourmet restaurant. One can only wonder what might happen to the desirability ratings of cooking and child rearing if homemakers were paid a decent daily wage.

Many people are physically sickened by the image of doctors as they perform surgery on their patients or, worse yet, conduct an autopsy. More than a few neophyte medical students have been known to go rubbery at the sight of a cadaver being anatomized. Yet Americans would hardly identify the role of doctor with dirty work. Instead, physicians continue to enjoy extremely high status with the American public, invariably being ranked ahead of most other occupations with respect to prestige. Apparently, even the most repulsive job is not necessarily thought of as dirty work. Is it a doctor's life-and-death struggle that makes the difference? In part, perhaps. But high income, prestige, and power can usually be counted on to turn the dirtiest work into good, clean fun! ∎

Suggestions for Further Reading

In "Who's Minding the Kids?" I suggest that the peer group has filled a void left by the absence of other strong institutions. To see the long-term trend in the rise of the peer group in relation to changes in the family, I recommend David Riesman's, *The Lonely Crowd* (1950). Even with the passage of decades, this classic work continues to teach us about American social character. Riesman sees the major source of socialization having changed with larger shifts in social character from tradition-directed to inner-directed to other-directed types. Until mid-20th century, parents continued to be the primary agents of socialization for youngsters. Children internalized a set of normative criteria during their early years that remained with them for life to guide their behavior. More recently, however, parents were replaced by the peer group as the major source of values and norms. Many youngsters became motivated not to please their parents but to gain the approval of their friends, associates, or contemporaries. They acted not so much out of an internal sense of what was right and wrong but more out of a desire to do what the peer group believed to be right and wrong.

"Let the System Do It!" focuses attention on the rise of specialized institutions, which, for the sake of efficiency, may have reduced the psychological burden of death and illness in our daily lives. German sociologist Max Weber long ago discussed this trend in modern society when he wrote about "rationalization"—the process whereby our lives have become increasingly dominated by institutions dedicated to efficiency and to the domination of human beings by technology. Weber recognized that we pay a price for this efficiency: the dehumanization of everyday life. For a discussion of Weber's treatment of rationalization, see Stephen Kalberg's "Max Weber's Types of Rationality: Cornerstones for the Analysis of Rationalization Processes in History," in the *American Journal of Sociology* (1980). Two excellent recent books by George Ritzer analyze modern life using Weber's concept of rationalization: *The McDonaldization of Society* (1993), about the fast-food industry, and *Expressing America* (1995), about our use of credit cards.

To read more about the changing situation of diversity on campus, see Howard J. Ehrlich's *Campus Ethnoviolence and the Policy Options* (1990). For a detailed analysis of violence against lesbians and gays, read the range of articles contained in Gregory Herek and Kevin Berrill's reader, *Hate Crimes: Confronting Violence Against Lesbians and Gay Men* (1992). Gary D. Comstock's *Violence Against Lesbians and Gay Men* (1991) provides research data and many interesting insights. One is worth repeating here: Whereas attacks against the members of different races are usually committed by economically marginal teenagers, violence against gays seems to come from every socioeconomic level.

Concerning "Dirty Work," I drew much of my discussion from an earlier project with Bill Levin, *The Functions of Discrimination and Prejudice* (1982). Sociologist Everett Hughes investigates a particularly hideous form of dirty work in an article in *Social Problems* titled "Good People and Dirty Work" (1962). In this article, Hughes attempted to come to grips with the factors that led otherwise ordinary Germans to work in concentration camps during the Nazi regime. Dirty work as part of the division of labor in a society, what Emile Durkheim calls "organic solidarity," can be seen in Durkheim's classic book *The Division of Labor in Society*, which he wrote in 1933.

■ **DEVELOPING IDEAS** *About Institutions*

1. Writing topic: Imagine that all institutions suddenly ceased to exist and that you personally had no choice but to take care of satisfying your own needs (and the needs of family members) on a daily basis. Write a short essay in which you describe a typical day in your life.

2. Writing topic: In a short essay, try to explain why students on campuses around the country are having so much trouble getting along with their schoolmates who are different. As indicated earlier, diversity on campus is on the rise. Do you sense that the level of competition—for popularity, status, grades, grants, scholarships, and jobs—has become more fierce? Could this be a factor in explaining the rise of intergroup hostility among college students? Before writing, you might want to jump ahead in this book and read through the snapshot about "The Economic Escalator" under the section on Social Inequality. Certainly, the educational institution has changed in important ways. Students attending colleges and universities in the

1960s were far less likely to work part-time while attending classes on a full-time basis. They were also less concerned about finding a good job after they graduated—after all, Americans enjoyed an unparalleled level of prosperity during the 1960s, and optimism abounded—at least among those who were fortunate enough to graduate from college.

3. Research topic: What is a family and what is not? To study the range of family conceptions held by college students, construct a short questionnaire and give it to a small sample of students on your campus. One approach would be for you to give your respondents a list of possible family arrangements that you develop beforehand and then ask them to evaluate as a legitimate family form. For example, you might include (a) mother, father, and children; (b) mother and children; (c) father and children; (d) mother, boyfriend, and children; (e) father, girlfriend, and children; (f) gay couple and children; (g) mother, stepfather, and children; (h) woman living alone; (i) college roommates; (j) grandparents and grandchildren; and so on.

4. Writing topic: In a short essay, discuss changes in the structure and functions of the family over the last 30 years. If you have completed the research topic above, how do you think your respondents would have answered the same question about family 30 years ago?

5. Research topic: Traditionally, garbage collecting has been viewed as dirty work, not only because it was physically unclean but also because it was a low-paying job. Collecting garbage is still physically dirty, but is it still low paying? To see how the dirtiness of garbage collecting may have changed over the years, compare the average income of garbage collectors in your town or state, or nationally, now versus 10, 20, and 30 years ago. Also determine whether the collectors are unionized and how often they have threatened to strike. If it is possible and makes sense, compare the racial or ethnic composition of garbage collectors over time. Why might you expect change in race or ethnic group? As a final possibility, examine in detail the circumstances of any strike that might have occurred among garbage collectors in your town. How long did it last? Just how much were garbage pickups missed during the strike? Did the strike disrupt business or school? How was the strike resolved?

PART FIVE

Deviance

The last time I visited a state prison, it was to interview a notorious serial killer. As you might expect, our conversation
began in a rather tentative manner. I tried to figure out what he
was thinking; he tried to figure out what I was up to. I sized him
up; he sized me up. Our first 30 minutes together consisted of an
exchange of polite trivialities. We talked about most everything—
everything, that is, except what I had come to discuss in the first
place: the heinous crimes for which he had been convicted.

If you've ever visited a prison, you probably know how uncomfortable it can be to talk with inmates, at least initially. There is
usually a great deal of anxiety, and it gets in the way of honest
communication.

Part of the problem involves what sociologist Erving Goffman
referred to as "the management of spoiled identity." An imprisoned serial murderer has been stigmatized; he is totally discredited among those who live beyond the prison walls. He knows that
I know; and I know that he knows that I know. There is no way for
him to conceal the fact that he has been found guilty of murdering
12 young women, even if he continues to proclaim his innocence
(which serial killers almost always do). The prison walls tell it all.
So the best we can expect to do is to minimize the discomfort generated by his deviance—and that takes both time and effort.

Deviance refers to any behavior of an individual that violates the
norms and values of a group or society generally. Many acts of
deviance are rather harmless—for example, parking in a loading
zone or breaking a curfew. Other acts of deviance are incredibly
dangerous and violent. When someone commits a severely deviant
act, he or she may be stigmatized. In other words, the violation of
society's rules is regarded as so extreme that an entire human being, and not just a particular behavior, gets discredited. Clearly,
serial killers fit this category. But as suggested in "Fat Chance in a
Slim World," so do individuals who are overweight by conventional standards—and they haven't broken any laws at all! "Fat" is
too often regarded as a symptom of not just illness but also a lack
of moral fiber or willpower. To some extent, people who are "too"
short, tall, or thin also bear the burden.

Mentally ill patients represent another group of stigmatized people. Some very depressed individuals would rather conceal their
pain and suffering than risk being rejected by the important people in their lives. As suggested in "You Must Get Ill First; Then

You Recover," those mental patients who are hospitalized also risk labeling. According to Erving Goffman, they may be thoroughly resocialized so that they can be easily managed and controlled. Goffman contends that new patients learn quickly what is required of them to get along while institutionalized and later to be released. Rosenhan's experiment in the same essay indicates clearly what happens when mental patients refuse to cooperate—they continue to be regarded as sick.

French sociologist Émile Durkheim once observed that deviant behavior actually helps to unite the members of a society by focusing attention on the validity of its moral order. In the face of a deviant act—for example, a heinous crime—the members of a group feel challenged, even threatened. They no longer take for granted the important values that they share. Instead, they rally their forces to encourage and support the legitimacy of "behaving correctly." Durkheim also suggested that punishing the individual who commits a deviant act similarly reconfirms behavior that conforms to a group's cultural standards. Punishment sends a message to every member of society: "Listen, buddy. Break the rules and the same thing will happen to you!"

Numerous Americans, concerned about our soaring crime rate, would gladly base their support of capital punishment on Durkheim's view of deviance: Sending a killer to the electric chair also sends a message to potential killers everywhere. Thus, capital punishment is often justified by the fact that it might serve as a *deterrent* to violent crime. As indicated in "Is the Death Penalty Only a Vehicle for Revenge?" however, there is very little evidence to suggest that capital punishment actually deters future murders (although it definitely deters the condemned killer from killing again). Even if most Americans favor capital punishment, most criminologists seem to agree that the *swift* and *certain* imposition of a life sentence without parole is an effective alternative to the death penalty. First-degree murderers should never be eligible for parole or furlough, and their sentences should never be commuted by a future governor who believes in their rehabilitation. As criminologist James A. Fox and I have argued, "We need a 'life sentence without hope.' "

Let me pause, at this point, to once again raise the question of "value-free" sociology. In "Is the Death Penalty Only a Vehicle for Revenge?" I take a definite stand—based on evidence collected by criminologists—but nevertheless a definite stand on a controversial issue. You should be aware that some sociologists would cringe at the very thought. In their view, the advocacy role is antithetical to the goals of the "science of sociology." Not everyone would agree, however. Sociologist Howard Becker has in fact argued just the opposite; that sociologists must take sides in favor of important values and pressing concerns. For him, the advocacy role is not only consistent with but essential to the work of sociology.

I am especially sure that the death penalty would have little impact on mass murderers. Those who kill several victims at a time would hardly be deterred by either a life sentence or an execution. Indeed, their killing spree is usually an act of suicide anyway; but before taking their own life, they have decided to get even with all of those individuals they blame for having caused their problems— *all* women, *all* foreigners, *all* postal workers, and so on.

Historically, the death penalty has been discriminatory in its application. For crimes of equivalent severity, black defendants were more likely than their white counterparts to be executed by the state. In 1972, the Supreme Court declared the death penalty unconstitutional because it was being applied in an uneven, capricious manner. In 1976, it was reinstated but only if applied under strict guidelines. Even today, there is evidence that the administration of the death penalty is uneven. Offenders who kill white victims "get the chair" more often than those offenders who kill black victims.

"Mass Murder: Summer's Fatal Time Bomb" indicates that the rate of horrific crime varies with climate, and I don't mean the weather. It is more likely the "social climate"—what happens when individuals interact—that seems to account for monthly variations in the level of mass murder. During the hot summer months, people get together more and their conversations heat up! ∎

Fat Chance in a Slim World
We Believe It's the Size of a Book's Cover That Counts

A black woman in Philadelphia recently wrote complaining about the way she was treated by other people. Among other things, she rarely dated, had few friends, and was forced to settle for a job for which she was overqualified. Moreover, passengers on buses and trains often stared at her with pity or scorn, while workers at the office rarely included her in their watercooler conversations.

The letter writer attributed these difficulties not to her gender or race but to the fact that she was vastly overweight by conventional standards. Her letter brought to mind the unfortunate victims of illnesses such as cancer, heart disease, and Alzheimer's disease who have the unavoidable symptoms of an illness over which they have little, if any, control. But they are typically treated with compassion and sympathy.

Curiously enough, fat people frequently receive contempt rather than compassion, unless their obesity can be attributed to some physical ailment (e.g., a "glandular condition"). Otherwise, they are seen as having caused their own problem by some combination of excessive impulsivity and lack of moral fiber. Not unlike prostitutes, ex-cons and homeless people, they may be regarded as lacking in the self-control and willpower necessary to lead a healthy, normal life. In addition, this discrimination has been directed more often at women than at men over the years.

The term *fat person* is therefore more than a description of somebody's weight, body type, or illness; more often than not, it is also used to stigmatize or discredit an entire group of human beings by making their belt size an excuse for bigotry. The lady from Philadelphia may have been correct: Research suggests that people who are overweight by our standards are often viewed as undesirable dates and mates. They frequently have trouble getting married, going to college, obtaining credit from a bank, or being promoted. In short, they are excluded, exploited, and oppressed.

Stigmatizing fat people is, of course, only one expression of a much more general tendency in our culture: the tendency to judge others by their looks rather than their intelligence, talent, or character. Study after study suggests that "what is beautiful is good!" That is, attractive individuals are more likely to be preferred as dates, to be popular with their friends, to be cuddled and kissed as newborns, to achieve high grades in school, to be disciplined less severely by their parents, to be recommended for a job after a personal interview, and to have their written work judged favorably.

By conventional American wisdom, fat is as ugly and deviant as thin is beautiful. We are so infatuated with being slim and trim that it is indeed hard to imagine anything else. Yet the desirability of particular body types and body weight varies from culture to culture. Beginning with the ancient world, fat has not always been universally despised. Instead, fat people were often respected, if not admired, throughout history. Even Cleopatra was fat by our standards, although by the standards of her own time and culture, she was a raving beauty. Renoir's French impressionist masterpieces similarly portrayed a version of the female body that today would be considered massive, huge, and fat rather than beautiful. And in cultures where food was in short supply, obesity was often used to validate personal success. Under such circumstances, rich people could afford to eat enough to be fat and therefore to survive. Skinny was therefore a sign of neither good health nor beauty but a symptom of poverty and illness.

Until the Roaring Twenties, the large and voluptuous version of feminine beauty continued to dominate in our culture. But the flappers changed all this by bobbing their hair, binding their breasts and, by some accounts, trying to resemble "adolescent boys." While many women of the 1920s moved toward feminine power, others retreated from it by shrinking their bodies in fad diets. The result was that during this era, the suffragette movement succeeded and women got the vote, but many men felt threatened. All of a sudden, they preferred women who were small, petite, and thin, who looked powerless.

Given the importance of physical attractiveness in defining the value and achievement of females, it should come as no surprise that American women have come under extreme pressure to be unrealistically slim and trim. This may have made many women dissatisfied with their bodies and mistakenly convinced them that mastery was possible only by controlling their weight. Women constitute 90% of those afflicted with the eating disorder anorexia nervosa and are the majority of those who join organizations such as Weight Watchers and Diet Workshop. Women are also more likely than men to suffer from compulsive overeating and obesity.

Since the women's movement of the 1960s, we seem to have become even more preoccupied with being slim and trim. *Playboy*'s centerfolds and contestants in the Miss America pageant have become increasingly thin. Leading women's magazines publish more and more articles about diets and dieting. Physicians offer drastic medical "cures," such as stomach stapling for obesity and liposuction surgery for "problem areas" like "saddlebag" thighs, "protuberant" abdomens, buttocks, "love handles," fatty knees, and redundant chins. And the best-seller list inevitably contains a disproportionate number of books promising miraculous methods of weight reduction.

In the face of all this, signs of an incipient cultural rebellion against crash dieting and irrational thinness have emerged. Popular books such as Millman's *Such a Pretty Face*, Orbach's *Fat Is a Feminist Issue*, and Chernin's *The Obsession: Reflections on the Tyranny of Slenderness* have taken their place in bookstores alongside the diet manuals. But rather than urge obedience to the conventional standards of beauty, these new books expose the dangers to physical and mental health due to rapid and repeated weight loss. Rather than focus on individual change, they place the blame for our excessive concern with being skinny on sexism and the socialization of women to absurd cultural standards.

The merchants of fashion have also sensed a cultural change in the offing. Growing numbers of dress shops now specialize in "designer fashions for size 14 and over" and "flattering designs in better plus size fashions." Moreover, based on a good deal of evidence from around the world, physicians have revised their weight standards so that what was formerly considered 10 or 15 pounds overweight is now regarded as optimal.

As a final element in this dynamic, organizations such as the National Association to Aid Fat Americans (NAAFA) have helped fat people—even those who are considered obese—to gain a more favorable self-image. Rather than automatically advising its members to diet, NAAFA calls attention to the fact that fat people are often the victims of prejudice and discrimination. It recognizes the dangers in rapid and repeated weight loss and focuses instead on improving the way that fat people are treated on the job, as customers, and in social situations. Taking its cue from black organizations, which reject words originating in the white community, such as *Negro* and *colored*, NAAFA prefers to use the term *fat* rather than *overweight* or *obese*. In this way, it refuses to conceal the issue in euphemisms, refuses to accept the stigma, and emphasizes that "fat can be beautiful!"

Unfortunately, however, our culture continues to give fat people a double message. On the one hand, we advise them to be themselves and to accept their body image regardless of social pressures to conform to some arbitrary standard of beauty. On the other hand, we urge them to go on a diet so that they will no longer be deviant. While the rhetoric may be confusing, it is also revealing. All things considered, our aversion is deeply embedded in our culture and is likely to remain with us for some time to come. ∎

You Must Get Ill First; Then You Recover

Checking Out of a Mental Hospital May Be Harder
Than Checking In

Sociologist Erving Goffman's study of the way patients were treated in a mental hospital yielded some frightening conclusions. He found that the hospital staff assumed absolute power to define how patients should think and behave. The institution gained total control over the terms by which its patients defined themselves. Inmates were thoroughly resocialized so that they could be easily managed and controlled.

According to Goffman, new patients learned quickly what was required of them to get along while institutionalized and later to be released. They were asked to discard their old self-concepts—those they had used "on the outside"—and to adopt a new set of self-definitions taught by the staff. First and foremost, inmates were to abandon the normal concept that they were "sane" or "healthy" and instead see themselves as "sick" and therefore in need of help. Admitting that they were psychologically ill was regarded as a patient's first step along "the road to recovery." Conversely, any claim that an inmate was "well" was regarded as a symptom of severe mental disease.

As patients spent more and more time in the hospital, larger areas of their self-concept were "turned upside down." Boredom was regarded as a sign of depression, anger as "acting out," independence as rebelliousness and irrationality, and a desire for privacy as withdrawal. It took no time at all for inmates to recognize that being resocialized by the institution to accept the role of a mentally ill person was the only way to be rewarded while confined and then later regarded as cured. This meant not being a management problem for the staff—submitting to the hospital routines, which included cooperation in taking medications and going to therapy sessions. Otherwise, a patient might remain in the institution indefinitely.

Ideally, of course, whether a patient is defined by the hospital staff as healthy or sick and viewed as ready for release should be based strictly on his or her symptoms. In reality, however, the social setting of a mental hospital also comes into play in defining the situation. This brings up an interesting question that sounds very much like the plot from an old movie: If perfectly normal and healthy people were secretly admitted to a mental hospital, would they be able to convince the staff that they were well, that they didn't belong, that they should be released? Or would they be defined by the rules of hospital life as rebellious, irrational, depressed, and therefore in need of continuing hospitalization?

A classic study by D. L. Rosenhan looked at exactly this question. He had eight sane individuals—five men and three women representing a range of ages and occupations—secretly admitted to a any one of a number of mental hospitals across the country. Each of Rosenhan's "pseudopatients" was totally free of any symptoms of mental illness; all of them gained admission by complaining that they "had been hearing voices." No hospital staff members were informed about the study.

Based only on this one symptom, hearing voices, all but one of the pseudopatients were diagnosed as suffering from schizophrenia. Moreover, once inside the hospital, the pseudopatients stopped expressing any symptoms of illness. They spoke and behaved normally for the entire duration of their stay.

When the pseudopatients expressed their desire to be discharged, they were told that release depended on the ability of a patient to convince the staff that he or she was sane. Yet despite their normal behavior, the average length of hospitalization for the group was 19 days. One of them failed to be released for 52 days. Finally, all of the pseudopatients were discharged—but with a diagnosis of "schizophrenia in remission." In other words, not one was able to convince a hospital staff of their sanity, only that the symptoms of their illness had subsided.

In case you were wondering whether *anyone*—staff or not—would have been fooled by Rosenhan's band of pseudopatients, we have an answer for you. Believe it or not, some 25% of the other patients on the admissions wards accused the pseudopatients of faking insanity—the real patients guessed that the imposters were actually professors or reporters who were in the hospital to conduct a study! ■

Is the Death Penalty Only a Vehicle for Revenge?

An Ardent Abolitionist States His Case

Whenever I articulate my opposition to the death penalty, I feel like a voice in the wilderness. Almost 86% of all Americans favor the death penalty; and the remaining 14% would probably be willing to make an exception if it meant eliminating the Ted Bundys of the world. In fact, the United States has the dubious distinction of being the only remaining Western nation not to have abolished the death penalty for civil homicide.

The reason underlying our overwhelming support of executions, according to a recent survey conducted for *ABC News* and the *Washington Post*, is usually revenge or retribution. Americans believe that the most serious crimes deserve the most severe punishment. As the Old Testament points out, "Thou shalt give life for life, eye for eye, tooth for tooth."

And I admit, it's not hard to understand why revenge seems sweet. People are fed up with violent crime, believing that it is out of control and of epidemic proportions. They want to do something about it. Many idolize Bernard Goetz, the so-called subway vigilante, because he refused to passively accept his victimization. The same appeal can be seen cinematically in Charles Bronson's *Death Wish* and in Sylvester Stallone's portrayal of Rambo and Rocky. Whether or not I agree with the extremity of the public reaction, I can understand why Bundy's execution by the state of Florida was seen by many as a cause for celebration. The world lost one of its most despicable killers.

The arguments for the death penalty, however, typically fall outside the realm of empirical inquiry. Instead, they are often emotionally charged, arguing that convicted killers deserve to die or that "getting even" is valuable as a measure of psychological compensation for victims and society. As an abolitionist, however, I rest my entire case on the weight of economic and social issues that can be demonstrated by empirical inquiry. These three important issues involve cost, deterrence, and protection.

Many people ask why we should spend hard-earned taxpayer money to imprison a murderer when we could just as easily execute him at much lower cost. But the fixed costs of running a maximum-security prison are little affected by the presence of a few additional inmates serving life sentences for first-degree murder. The warden still has to be paid and the heat still has to be kept on. Moreover, because of the lengthy appeals process required by the Supreme Court in capital cases, it actually costs less to imprison a killer than to execute one. In Florida, for example, the average cost of a case that results in execution is $3.2 million, whereas the estimated cost of imprisonment for 40 years is slightly more than $500,000. And to those who argue, "If it costs so much to carry out the appeals process, then take him out back and string him up," consider the number of errors that have been made under less stringent requirements: Since 1900, 139 people have been sent to death who were later proven innocent. Twenty-three of them were exonerated only after the executions had been carried out. In addition, the typical length of imprisonment between sentencing and execution is actually only 3 years, not the 11 years that Ted Bundy manipulated out of the court system.

Proponents of the death penalty also claim that it deters violent criminals. They believe we need to execute murderers to send messages to potential killers that, if they can't control their murderous behavior, the same thing will happen to them.

Yet the death penalty has little if any effect on killings. In a study of 14 nations in which the death penalty was eliminated, criminologists Dane Archer and Rosemary Gartner report, for example, that abolition was followed more often than not by a reduction in national homicide rates. For example, homicide dropped 59% in Finland, 30% in Italy, 63% in Sweden, and 46% in Switzerland. In only 5 of these 14 countries did homicide increase at all. Even more ironically, research conducted by criminologist William Bowers suggests that the murder rate actually rises for a short period of time after the killer has been executed, producing what he calls a "brutalization effect." That is, would-be murderers apparently identify more with the state executioner than they do with the inmate.

The third argument, of course, is that capital punishment protects society by guaranteeing that killers like Charles Manson will never be paroled. And certainly, capital punishment would make sure that particular murderers never kill again. But before I support the death penalty, I want to know whether an alternative exists for protecting society—for making sure that a killer isn't granted another opportunity—without taking human life. If the alternative in response to a brutal, hideous murder is life imprisonment with parole eligibility, then I am indeed in favor of the death penalty. If, however, the alternative is a life sentence without the possibility of ever being paroled, then capital punishment becomes unnecessary for the protection of society, and I am therefore against it.

In fact, I cringe whenever I hear that Charles Manson is being considered for parole, because I know what people will say: "The criminal justice system is soft on murderers. We should be executing those who commit heinous crimes." Actually, Charles Manson did receive the death penalty. But in 1972, the Supreme Court struck down capital punishment because it was being applied in an uneven, capricious manner. At that point, any murderer on death row was instead given the next most severe sentence under state law. In California, that sentence was a life sentence with parole eligibility. As a result, Charles Manson was then eligible for parole after serving only 7 years.

A series of rulings by the Supreme Court in 1976 paved the way for states to restore the death penalty but only when applied under strict guidelines. In some states (for example, California), those convicted of murder continue to become eligible for parole after serving only several years in prison; but if the court adds the "special circumstances provision," the only possible sentences are either death or life imprisonment without parole eligibility.

Most states now have special circumstances statutes for heinous crimes, such as multiple murder or murder with rape. In some states (e.g., Massachusetts), all first-degree murderers are ineligible for parole, so that no special statute is required. Under such conditions, the death penalty is unnecessary as a means for protecting society from vicious killers, because we can instead lock them up and throw away the key.

Actually, many proponents of the death penalty raise the issues of cost, deterrence, and protection of society only to rationalize what essentially is a thirst for revenge. This can be seen most clearly in the public response to heinous crimes.

In December 1987, Ronald Gene Simmons brutally murdered 16 people in Russellville, Arkansas, in the largest family massacre in American history. When the residents of Russellville learned that

Simmons had suffocated the young children in his family and that he had had an incestuous relationship with his married daughter, cries for the death penalty were heard loud and clear throughout Arkansas. In 1989, Simmons was convicted of multiple murder and sentenced to die by means of lethal injection. Similarly, in October 1989, a young pregnant woman from Reading, Massachusetts, was shot to death by her husband, Charles Stuart. Public outrage quickly took the form of demands for Massachusetts legislators to enact a death penalty statute.

Florida certainly did get a measure of self-satisfaction by electrocuting serial killer Ted Bundy; the same can be said for the state of Illinois when it executed John Wayne Gacy, the notorious serial killer, in 1994. For many Americans, the opportunity to get even with a serial killer is reason enough to apply the death penalty. But for those few who instead believe that capital punishment can be justified only to the extent that it protects society's members or serves as an effective deterrent, then execution by the state is cruel and unnecessary punishment. In a civilized society, our best defense against "wild animals" is to lock them in cages so they can't get to the rest of us. ■

Mass Murder
Summer's Fatal Time Bomb

I hate to be a prophet of doom, but it is entirely conceivable—no, probable—that our local newspapers will soon carry the gruesome details of yet another massacre in the United States. My prediction is entirely feasible because there are at least 20 mass killings in the United States every year, and a disproportionate number of them occur during July and August.

This concentration of massacres during the summer is nothing new. Remember, it was August 1, 1966, when Charles Whitman climbed to the top of the tower at the University of Texas and fired on the crowd below. From that vantage point, he extinguished the lives of 14 and injured another 30 before being gunned down by police. More recently, James Huberty went "hunting for humans" in a San Ysidro, California, McDonald's on July 18, 1984. With his rifle, a shotgun, and a pistol, Huberty entered the fast-food restaurant and opened fire on patrons while they were eating lunch. Newspapers called it "the Big Mac Attack" and "Mass McMurder," but there was nothing funny about slaying 21 innocent victims. And three summers later, this time in August, a 23-year-old Vietnamese immigrant went on a shooting spree in Dorchester, Massachusetts, in a bloody act of retaliation against those he believed responsible for tarnishing his reputation. The young killer ended his own life but not before he had murdered five and wounded two others.

So if recent history repeats itself, we're in for big trouble this summer. Another random slaughter of strangers could take place on a street corner or in a crowded supermarket parking lot. Some distraught husband may massacre his family, taking them with him to the hereafter. Another mass murderer may gun down customers and employees during an armed robbery.

Why do so many massacres occur during the summer? The image of a crazed killer who is driven beyond the edge of sanity by excessive heat and humidity comes immediately to mind. It is an ancient belief that the weather has important effects on what we do and how we feel. The Greek philosopher Hippocrates talked about health in relation to changes of the seasons and the rising and setting of the stars. The Talmud suggests that certain illnesses are caused by standing nude under the spell of a full moon. Certainly, you wouldn't have trouble convincing astrology buffs or even the radio talkmasters who claim that every lunatic in town calls when the moon is full and the humidity rises.

Research even suggests that hot, muggy weather puts people in a bad mood. During an oppressive hot spell, customers in restaurants are less generous with tips, and witnesses are less likely to help others in an emergency. When the humidity rises, so do admissions to mental hospitals, harsh discipline and punishment in schools, and the suicide rate.

Clearly, then, weather has an influence on human behavior. Under extreme conditions, it might even serve as a precipitating event for violence. At the same time, however, it takes more than a few hot sticky days to create a mass murderer or even to push him or her over the edge.

In our book, *Mass Murder: America's Growing Menace*, criminologist James A. Fox and I studied 42 mass murderers who had each killed four or more victims between 1974 and 1979. We searched newspaper accounts, conducted telephone and personal interviews, and studied biographies and in-depth interviews with mass killers. We were also able to compare massacres with single-victim homicides by studying FBI information available on the 96,263 homicides in the United States for the years 1976 through 1980, including 156 incidents of mass murder.

In almost every case of mass murder, we discovered that the killer had experienced profound frustration in his personal life, often over a period of many years, if not decades. In addition, there was usually a precipitating event in the killer's life, much more than just a change in the weather. Instead, at some point prior to the mass murder, the killer had typically experienced the actual or threatened loss of a job or a loved one, causing him to become despondent and hopeless. We also learned that most mass murderers had access to and training in the use of firearms. This fact alone may explain why 95% of all mass killers are men; they have unequal access to weapons of mass destruction, having traditionally monopolized the military service, fields of law enforcement, and hunting as a hobby.

James Ruppert is an appropriate example. Like the majority of mass killers, Ruppert is a white, middle-aged male. In 1975, this resident of Hamilton, Ohio—at the time, 40 years old—was responsible for one of the worst mass murders in the history of the United

States; he shot to death 11 members of his family—his mother, his brother and sister-in-law, and their 8 children.

Ruppert had led a life of frustration, beginning with childhood. As a young boy, he was asthmatic, shy, and clumsy. He walked hunched over from illness, so sickly that he was not permitted to take gym at school or play sports with the neighborhood kids. In high school, he was teased or harassed by his schoolmates, never dating or participating in extracurricular activities. As an adult, he flunked out of college, had no sexual relations with women and drifted from job to job. And as if this weren't enough, Ruppert's mother threatened to evict him from the house in which they had lived together for many years unless he repaid his debts to her and stopped his excessive drinking. It was against this background that Ruppert came down the stairs of his mother's home carrying two handguns and a rifle for a few rounds of target practice on the banks of the local river. But before he reached the front door, he instead slaughtered his family.

More than the weather and factors of frustration, another element of mass murder may be based more on common sense than on behavioral science theory: During July and August, many people spend more time together, stay up later, and congregate on the streets and are therefore available to be killed simultaneously. For similar reasons, mass murder is also overrepresented during winter or anytime when family and friends come together for their annual holiday reunion, sometimes traveling great distances to be with their loved ones. Holidays heighten emotions, both positive and negative; they also provide an opportunity for killers to get even with everyone they believe has conspired against them.

In December 1987, for example, the largest family slaughter in United States history occurred in Dover, Arkansas, when Gene Simmons murdered 14 members of his family as they convened for their Christmas reunion. At any other time of the year, there would have been fewer family members available to massacre. A few days later, seven members of the Dreesman family were found shot to death in their Algona, Iowa, home. Four of them had traveled from Hawaii for the holiday and would probably still be alive if the murders had taken place in February or May. Also during December, there were mass killings in Long Beach, California; Dayton, Texas; Nashua, New Hampshire; and Wichita, Kansas. James Ruppert's 1975 massacre also occurred during an annual family reunion, on

Easter Sunday. If Ruppert had gotten angry on a Monday morning in June, probably only one person—his mother—would have died.

Because so many mass killings occur in July and August, during the hottest months of the year *and* during some of the coldest months of the year, it's not the weather per se, but changes in the way people interact during these periods that really make a difference. Sunny California, Texas, and Florida do have more than their share of mass murders—but so does New York. In all of these states, there are large numbers of transient, rootless people who have no place to turn when the frustrations of everyday life become intolerable. And despite their hot and humid climate, states in the Deep South have fewer mass killings than you would expect based on population alone. Unlike other regions of the country, Georgia, Mississippi, and Tennessee continue to have strong local institutions—family, religion, and fraternal organizations—that provide support and guidance when times get tough, therefore immunizing their residents against committing mass murder.

So consider yourselves warned. During July and August, people get together for pool parties, shopping sprees, and family barbecues. In many sections of the city, they attempt to recover from the heat of the day by staying up late, sitting together on the front stoop of their sweltering apartment houses and talking with their neighbors. The potential for anger, resentment, and argument can build; the potential for victimizing large numbers of people also escalates, simply because more people are available to kill simultaneously. For those reasons, we again may soon be reading the details of yet another gruesome killing—unless, of course, we are able to change the *social* climate. ∎

■ FOCUS *Suggestions for Further Reading*

In the introduction to this section, I discussed the work of French sociologist Émile Durkheim. The frequency with which he appears in this small book should suggest just how much the work of Durkheim has influenced the direction of sociology. Durkheim's views of crime are found in *The Rules of Sociological Method* (1966).

Concerning "Is the Death Penalty Only a Vehicle for Revenge?" my argument relies on numerous studies by criminologists, most of whom find little or no support for the death penalty. For a major study of capital punishment, read William J. Bowers's book *Executions in America* (1974). Dane Archer and Rosemary Gartner, in their important book titled *Violence and Crime in Cross-National Perspective* (1984), provide cross-national evidence. They found a *reduction* in homicide for most of the countries in which the death penalty was abolished.

My snapshot about the death penalty takes a controversial position. I first raised the issue of value-free sociology in the introduction to this book; it should come as no surprise to see it again—especially in discussing how to deal with crime. In 1918, Max Weber gave a lecture at Munich University concerning the importance of value-free sociology. You can find his speech reprinted in *Max Weber: Essays in Sociology*, edited by H. H. Gerth and C. Wright Mills (1946). For a different point of view regarding the place of values in sociological analysis, read "Whose Side Are We On?" by Howard S. Becker, in *Social Problems* (1967). He argues that sociological research is *always* biased, never value-free; in fact, every sociologist has a responsibility to take sides in support of important values and concerns.

Concerning the snapshot entitled "Mass Murder: Summer's Fatal Time Bomb," I relied heavily on research reported in two books I coauthored with James A. Fox. The first is called *Mass Murder: America's Growing Menace* (1991); the second is *Overkill: Mass Murder and Serial Killing Exposed* (1994). In our initial research, we examined 42 mass and serial killers. We subsequently studied FBI information concerning 137 offenders who had committed 156 incidents of mass murder. Concerning mass killers, you might also read Elliott Leyton's interesting work, *Compulsive Killers* (1986). Jack Katz examines the subjective experiences of "doing" crime in his fascinating book, *Seductions of Crime: Moral and Sensual Attrac-*

tions of Doing Evil (1988). He looks beyond the practical and sense-less motivational veneer of criminal behavior and focuses instead on its moral and sensual rewards. For a controversial and impor-tant explanation for criminal behavior, read Michael Gottfredson and Travis Hirschi's *A General Theory of Crime* (1990). Gottfredson and Hirschi present evidence for the position that an essential ele-ment in criminality is an absence of self-control, usually learned early in life.

Throughout this section, we have emphasized criminal behavior as a form of deviance. In closing this section, let me point out, once again, that crime is only one form of deviance and that devi-ance is actually a much broader concept. Many sociologists who specialize in deviance aren't primarily interested in crime at all and instead study various forms of deviant behavior, such as men-tal illness or physical disability.

In "Fat Chance in a Slim World," we are also told that, through-out history, people who would be considered overweight by Americans in the 1990s were instead respected, admired, and re-garded as attractive. Rather than the epitome of feminine beauty, even Cleopatra of ancient Egypt was fat by our standards!

In contrast, Americans who are overweight by conventional standards are stigmatized. Specifically, they are treated as lacking in moral fiber and character. As more "food for thought" about this topic, pick up Kim Chernin's interesting book, *The Obsession* (1981). She suggests that women's acceptance of society's increas-ing demand for females to be thin reflects cultural pressure for women to dislike their bodies. For Chernin, rigid dieting and boy-ish fashions are forms of rejection of feminine power and equality. My snapshot depends a good deal on Chernin and on Marcia Millman's excellent sociological treatise about being fat in Amer-ica, *Such a Pretty Face* (1980). For the classic sociological treatment of the presentation of "spoiled" self, see Erving Goffman's *Stigma: Notes on the Management of Spoiled Identity* (1963). While reading Goffman, think about the influence that being fat or skinny or very short or very tall can have on a child's self-image.

Goffman has also written extensively about mental hospitals. His book titled *Asylums* (1958) is a classic in the field. David Rosenhan's excellent study of normal people gaining entrance into a mental hospital and then asking to be discharged is reported in his 1973 article, "On Being Sane in Insane Places," appearing in

Science. For an excellent discussion of the social conditions implicated in mental illnesses such as depression and anxiety, read *Social Causes of Psychological Distress* (1989) written by John Mirowsky and Catherine Ross.

■ DEVELOPING IDEAS *About Deviance*

1. Writing topic: Max Weber urged sociologists to attempt to be objective, even when their personal views were being contradicted. Gun control is a controversial issue—there are many proponents on both sides. In writing, state your own personal opinion—either for or against the restriction of firearms as a national policy. Then, in a short essay, defend the point of view that *opposes* your own.

2. Research topic: Every year, the U.S. Department of Justice publishes the Uniform Crime Reports for the United States. In *Crime in the United States,* you will find a number of different statistics concerning the serious crimes reported to the FBI by local police departments. This book is easily available in libraries or from the U.S. Government Printing Office. Using *Crime in the United States* for a recent year, find monthly variations in murder and verify that murder rates peak during July, August, and December. Now, do the same for property crimes such as larceny theft and burglary. Do these offenses also peak during the relatively cold month of December? Why or why not? Explain how the "social climate" may have more influence than the weather on monthly variations in homicide. Do you think that the social climate has the same effect on property crimes?

3. Research topic: Based on public opinion surveys, we know that most Americans favor the death penalty. But we also know that support for capital punishment decreases if people see an alternative that protects society just as well. For example, in a 1994 survey of Massachusetts citizens, William J. Bowers found that 54% prefer life without parole over the death penalty. Now, it's your turn. In a paper-and-pencil questionnaire, ask 20 students to indicate whether they support or oppose capital punishment. Now, also ask the supporters of the death penalty to indicate whether they would support or oppose it under the following

conditions: (a) if life imprisonment were the only alternative sentence available; (b) if life imprisonment without parole eligibility were the only alternative sentence available; (c) if "life without hope"—that is, life imprisonment without parole eligibility, pardon, or commutation of sentence were the only alternative available; or (d) if life imprisonment without parole eligibility plus victim restitution were the only alternative sentence available. What do your results indicate about "protection of society" as a motivation for supporting the death penalty?

4. Research topic: With your instructor's assistance, commit an act of deviance to see how others respond to you. Select an act that is neither illegal nor unethical. Also, make sure that your deviant behavior will not affect the way you are treated by others on a permanent basis! Because it isn't always so easy to think of a "safe" act of deviance, let me suggest one. Simply mark your forehead with a meaningless symbol—for example, two blue and red circles. Then, walk on campus and observe the reactions (or lack of reactions). Do strangers and friends respond differently to you? Finally, try the same experiment, but this time walk on campus with two other students whose foreheads have been painted like yours. Do you notice a difference in the way you are treated? What do you think people assume when they encounter three students wearing the same unknown symbol?

5. Research topic: Interview an individual who seems to be stigmatized because of his or her appearance (someone considered fat, short, tall, unattractive, and so on). In your interview, try to determine at what age your respondent first remembers being "different." Have your respondent indicate the specific ways in which he or she has been discriminated against—at work, on dates, at school. Also try to discover how he or she manages the stigma (denial or avoidance?). Note: Please be careful not to approach a stigmatized person in a hurtful or insensitive way. You might want to place an ad in your college newspaper asking for volunteers who have been labeled as too short, too tall, or too fat. Or you might invite volunteers from among your classmates. It may even be possible to locate an organization to which stigmatized people belong—for example, Little People of America or the National Association to Aid Fat Americans. In

any case, it is obviously important to use extreme sensitivity in locating a potential respondent.

6. Writing topic: Name a group in American society, other than "fat" people, whose members have been stigmatized. How do you think they would be treated in some other culture? Why?

7. Research topic: Walk around for one day as a fat person to see how other people treat you. With the help of a friend, put on more than a few pounds—literally put on weight by wearing large clothing and padding yourself in a realistic way. Then, take written notes as to any differences you detect in the reactions of others.

PART SIX

Social Inequality

"**C**an you spare some change for a cup of coffee, mister?" I never know what to do when I am confronted by a panhandler asking for a handout, especially if he looks like he's been drinking. If I give him what he wants, I might only be supplying him with his next drink of booze—and his next hangover. But if I don't give him anything, I feel guilty. Who knows, maybe he hasn't eaten in 3 days and my small contribution will keep him going until the next handout comes along.

Homeless people in the streets of our major cities represent an extreme example of *social inequality*—the unequal distribution of wealth, power, and prestige among the members of society. At the other end of that distribution, there are entertainers and professional athletes who earn millions of dollars a year, enjoy tremendous popularity, and have a great deal of pull. In between the panhandler and the famous ballplayer, most of us fall.

Clearly, we are not a classless society. In fact, social inequality in America is highly structured and passed from one generation to another. This characteristic of social inequality is known as *social stratification*. In fact, social inequality is definitely stratified. Sociologists have been able to identify a number of different social classes whose members share similar occupational positions, opportunities, attitudes, and lifestyles—an upper class containing the wealthiest and most powerful people in America, an upper-middle class consisting of the families of business executives and professionals who have high income, a lower-middle class consisting of average-income Americans, a working class containing primarily blue-collar workers, and a lower class consisting of the "disreputable poor."

Life chances is Max Weber's term referring to an individual's probability of securing the "good things of life." Sociologists are well aware that an individual's life chances definitely vary by social class. Regardless of their intelligence and steadfastness, people who are born into a low social class will likely benefit less from society's opportunities than people born into a higher social class. Members of lower classes are *less* likely to vote, obtain favors from politicians, go to college, receive adequate public services, be in good physical and mental health, have decent working conditions, or feel they have control over their everyday lives. They are *more* likely to give birth out of wedlock, grow up in single-parent families, be arrested and imprisoned after committing a crime, and die at an early age.

Many observers have suggested that the gap between rich and poor has widened over the period of the last decade or so. Clearly, there are now more homeless people on the streets of our major cities and more middle-class families whose members have "skidded" in terms of social class. In "The Economic Escalator," we find that intergenerational mobility seems to be in a downward direction. Consequently, millions of young people have begun to question the validity of the American Dream. Young adults have been particularly hard hit. As a result, they are staying in school longer, delaying their marriage plans, and moving back in with their parents.

Social inequality varies by gender, race, and age. African Americans continue to be disproportionately represented in poverty. Affirmative action legislation may have helped create a large and viable black middle class, but it has hardly touched the lives of the members of the black underclass who continue to live in permanent poverty. In our postindustrial society, we lack the jobs that could propel young black males out of the underclass. And where such jobs do exist, they tend to be low-paying jobs that lead nowhere.

In addition, American women continue to earn less than their male counterparts. Moreover, when both husband and wife hold full-time jobs, it is usually the working woman who is expected to do the household chores and child rearing as well. She continues to be the main source of advice and guidance for her children and the one who is held responsible for cleaning and cooking. Perhaps this fact of life helps explain the American female's disadvantage on the job: Because of the extra burden placed on her shoulders, the working woman is often unable to make the same commitment to her career that her husband can.

In the early 1980s, we were in the grip of a recession, and older Americans suffered more than their share of economic hardship. Some were eating dog food to survive. Perhaps fewer elders are now in critical economic condition, but their image continues to give them problems. In "Images of Aging," I suggest that the old stereotype that all older people are poor, sickly, and incompetent has been joined by a new stereotype that they are *also* powerful and wealthy—perhaps too powerful and wealthy for their own good. The new view may turn out to be particularly dangerous, inspiring conflict between the generations for increasingly scarce economic resources. Indeed, there already exist political pressure organizations designed to minimize the influence of older people in the area of social security and health care. Americans for Generational Equity represents the interests of young people, and the American Association of Boomers represents the interests of middle-aged Americans.

The United States is in the midst of a possibly unprecedented period of immigration—and not everyone is delighted. In "The Functions of Immigrant Bashing," I discuss the violence perpetrated against newcomers not only in the United States but around the world, as increasing numbers of frustrated individuals look for someone to blame for their declining economic situation. Using the framework laid out by sociologist Lewis Coser in his modern classic, *The Functions of Social Conflict*, I also raise the possibility that immigrant bashing helps protect the leaders of a society from the unmitigated hostility of its citizens.

How do we explain the fact that poverty is overrepresented among Black Americans? Do we blame racism? Job loss? Family structure? Or . . . In "Race, IQ, and Hysterectomies," I examine the controversial hypothesis that racial groups differ with respect to intelligence. Rather than enter the debate, however, I examine the debaters, the psychologists who express an opinion that blacks are, on average, genetically inferior to whites in terms of intelligence. If the link between race and IQ were objective science, psychologists' age and region would have no effect on the position that they draw regarding the controversy. Without giving away the "punch line," let me simply suggest that scientists are human beings, too. They are influenced by where they grow up, what their parents have told them is right and wrong, and what their friends believe. ∎

The Economic Escalator
Americans on Their Way Down

The term *downward mobility* is used to characterize the economic plight of an entire generation of middle-class Americans who are slipping and sliding their way down the socioeconomic ladder. Forget about the short-term effects of recession. According to political analyst Kevin Phillips, the culprit is an economic trend that began in the 1980s and will likely continue indefinitely.

The rich really have been getting much richer—and apparently doing so at the expense of poor and middle-income Americans who have seen their status evaporate. Through at least the last decade, the biggest losers have been blacks, Latinos, young men, female heads of households, farmers, and steelworkers; but almost everyone else has also suffered to some extent.

In a shift away from manufacturing toward services, we have been transformed into a postindustrial society. In 1959, production of goods represented some 60% of all American employment, but by 1985, this figure had dropped to only 26%. The overwhelming majority of Americans are now employed in the service sector of the economy. During this transitional period, new jobs were created, but in the main, these were poorly paid and provided few opportunities for upward mobility. Large numbers of Americans were forced to take a substantial drop in pay and, therefore, in their way of life.

According to Phillips, the widening gap between rich and poor may have been encouraged by national economic policies of the 1980s, a period that represented a strong reversal of almost four decades of downward income redistribution. At the upper end of our class system, the after-tax proportion of income for the wealthiest 1% of Americans climbed from 7% in 1977 to 11% in 1990. Even when adjusted for inflation, the number of millionaires doubled between the late 1970s and the late 1980s, resulting in a record 1 million households reporting a net worth of at least $1 million.

For families on lower rungs of the socioeconomic ladder, however, living standards have deteriorated. Since 1977, the average after-tax family income of the bottom 10% of Americans declined 10.5% in current dollars. According to a recent study by Professor Timothy Smeeding of Syracuse University, the percentage of U.S. children living in poverty rose from less than 15% in 1978 to 20% today. Compared with seven other industrial countries (Sweden, West Germany, Australia, Canada, Britain, France, and the Netherlands), the United States has the dubious distinction of being the most unequal. That is, we have more poverty and fewer people who are middle class.

Growing income inequality has already been linked with a worsening of our most stubborn and perplexing social ailments. Professor Henry Miller of the University of California notes that homelessness is a growing problem in our major cities—a problem that is not susceptible to easy solutions.

He suggests that we were previously able as a society to assimilate many of the homeless into the military or industry. In today's economy, however, those who lack education or marketable skills remain permanently unemployed or take dead-end jobs. What is more, in the process of converting inexpensive rooming houses into high-priced condominiums for the affluent, the gentrification of urban areas during the 1980s forced even more of the poverty stricken onto the streets.

According to *American Demographics*, young adults have been particularly hard hit by downward mobility. As a result, they are taking longer to finish school, living for a longer period of time with their parents or other relatives, and delaying their plans to marry. Young married couples are today less likely to own their own homes. Many return to live with their parents.

Comparing their worsening economic circumstances with those of their parents, millions of young people have begun to question the validity of the American Dream and are less optimistic about the future. Called "selfish," "passive," and "ultraconservative" by those who remember the liberal activism of the prosperous 1960s, many young adults are merely trying to maintain or improve their standard of living. In the face of an erosion in their incomes, they frequently regard tax increases as a burden they cannot afford.

American business leaders are beginning to understand that America's economic problems have a long-term basis in reality. The Business Council, whose members consist of 100 executives from America's largest companies, suggested recently that the recent recession will be succeeded by a prolonged period of lean economic times. The public seems to agree: A recent *Business Week* survey determined that 64% of Americans predict that the economy of the

United States will be dominated by foreign companies within 10 years.

The continuing trends away from manufacturing and toward inequality between rich and poor are, of course, far from inevitable. But a reversal would necessitate a major commitment on the part of political leaders, business, and the public who recognize the urgency of finding a solution. The urban underclass is now at least four times larger than it was during the turbulent 1960s, when our major cities were burning. Disturbances have already begun to erupt in some major cities. Some predict that there will be riots of "earthquake" proportions within 2 to 3 years in at least four major cities: New York, Chicago, Los Angeles, and Miami. At that point, there will undoubtedly be widespread support for making essential changes in our economy. The real question is one of timing: Will we be too late? ∎

Images of Aging
Are the Elderly Too Powerful?

Several years ago, 80-year-old Clara Peller achieved overnight fame for her line in a Wendy's ad, "Where's the Beef?" Peller's comic portrayal of a cantankerous old lady reflects a familiar stereotype; older people are seen as entering a second childhood in which they become bossy, irritable, feeble, and possibly weakened in intellect and make large, unreasonable demands on others. With low incomes and high health costs, elderly consumers are seen as especially concerned about finding the "beef," about getting good value for their money.

Studies of age stereotyping conducted over the past 50 years show that this image of aging has been widely accepted. Gerontologists' research among graduate students of psychology in the 1950s shows that most believed that old people are set in their ways, walk slowly, have poor coordination, are bossy, and like to doze. These results have been duplicated in more recent research. A 1988 study by William C. Levin reported in *Research on Aging* showed that Americans characterize older people as less intelligent, competent, healthy, active, creative, attractive, reliable, energetic, flexible, educated, wealthy, and socially involved than younger people.

Most of my students routinely overestimate the percentage of the elderly who live below the poverty line or in nursing homes. For example, the average estimate was that 37% of all Americans 65 years or older are now residing in a nursing home, while the actual figure is only 4%.

Surprisingly, these same students also overestimated the percentage of senators, judges, and former presidents who were at least 65 and the proportion of billionaires, CEOs of major corporations, and corporate stockholders who are elderly. The same students who were unrealistic about poverty and dependence exaggerated the wealth and power of the elderly: Less than 5% of major American corporations are actually headed by a CEO who is 65 or older, but the average estimated by the students was 43%.

In this latter stereotype, older people are often seen as powerful and rich—perhaps too powerful and rich for their own good.

Traditionally, older people were blamed for their own plight; their poverty and dependence were regarded as an inevitable part of the life cycle. In the new view, however, the aged are seen as having disproportionate influence in the government, as having garnered too large a share of the country's economic resources, and as responsible for a national debt of unprecedented proportions and for health care costs that seem to be out of control.

The former view long justified encouraging the elderly to disengage from work, despite evidence that older workers are as productive as their younger counterparts.

The new stereotype is potentially even more dangerous. It justifies organizing against the interests of the elderly, cutting the government expenditures that benefit them, perhaps even eliminating Social Security, and reducing efforts to keep the aged alive. In this view, since the elderly have so much wealth and political clout, they do not need the help of younger Americans.

Some have already begun to exploit the new stereotype. In politics, the interests of the elderly and the young have been pitted against one another as though they were in essential conflict—a substitute for the real battle that is so carefully avoided—that of the poor and middle class against the rich. Americans for Generational Equity (AGE), for example, argues that the status of the elderly has greatly improved at the expense of the well-being of the young. The leaders of AGE cite statistics showing high rates of poverty among children, a decline in real income among baby boomers, and a massive federal debt. AGE blames the elderly for consuming too much of the national budget and enjoying increases in Social Security benefits, while inflation-adjusted wages for the rest of the population have declined.

Even more disturbing is the extent to which this perception may be influencing medical personnel who make life and death decisions. Studies have shown that emergency room personnel tend to expend greater effort resuscitating younger patients. In 1984, Colorado's former governor Richard Lamm said that the elderly "have a duty to die" because of the financial cost of health care needed to prolong the lives of the elderly. According to Lamm, it might cost too much to keep them alive.

Now the Clara Peller image is of someone who has found the beef and refuses to share it with her grandchildren. Older Americans deserve a better commercial. ∎

The Functions of Immigrant Bashing
When Hospitality Turns Hostile

Voices of xenophobia and racism once again reverberate throughout German society, and concerned observers want to know why. East Germany has struggled to make the transition from Communism to a free market economy; but its high unemployment and inefficient use of resources have inspired violent attacks on refugees and workers from Eastern European and Third World countries. During 1991 alone, there were more than 1,500 attacks against foreigners. In September 1991, for example, 600 right-wing German youths fire-bombed a home for foreigners and then attacked 200 Vietnamese and Mozambicans in the streets of Hoyerswerde.

Even Western Germany has not been totally immune from the effects of economic tension, although episodes of violence have been far less severe and less frequent. In an apparent act of racially inspired arson, a 25-year-old Ghanaian was burned to death and his two Nigerian roommates seriously injured in a fire that swept through a hotel for foreigners seeking asylum in the city of Saarlouis.

Much of the violence in Germany has been perpetrated by a relatively small number of extremists—an estimated 5,000 hard-core neo-Nazis and another 30,000 racist skinheads. In East Berlin, a chapter of Neo-Nazis recruited only a few hundred unemployed and alienated young men who gave voice to racism and xenophobia as a way of "fighting back."

Yet the degree of resentment in Germany can be easily underestimated. Based on the results of a 1992 national poll, up to 40% of all German citizens can be characterized as "silent sympathizers." They express at least some sympathy for the issues—"Germany for Germans," "racial purity," and "foreigners out"—espoused by right-wing extremists. Moreover, 15% of Germany's youths say they now consider Adolph Hitler to be "a great man." In the underground computer game *Concentration Camp Manager*, the fine art of xenophobia takes a macabre twist. German high school students who play it are challenged by the task of killing as many Turks with as little gas as possible.

We must be careful not to view anti-immigrant sentiment as an exclusively "German problem." In reality, violence against foreigners has recently increased in countries around the world, mainly in response to a burgeoning presence of immigrant workers. Across the globe, millions are leaving their homelands for the sake of a better life—and they do not always receive a friendly welcome from the citizens of their host country.

Even in China, where foreigners have long enjoyed deferential treatment, there are signs that resentment against the 1,500 African students who study there is on the rise. Formerly minor incidents have become major points of conflict. For example, hearing that black African male students had taken Chinese women to a Christmas Eve dance, thousands of Chinese demonstrators amassed in the streets of Nanjing, shouting racial insults like "Beat the blacks."

In France, mounting resentment against its 2 million Muslim Arab immigrants has provoked the government to speed up the process of integrating newcomers into French society and to tighten controls against illegal immigration. In March 1990, three men of North African origin were brutally murdered in separate racially motivated attacks. Public opinion pollsters report that 76% of all French citizens now believe there are too many Arabs in their country.

In Italy, a traditional haven for newcomers, hospitality has similarly turned cold. Hardly a week passes without some episode of conflict between immigrants and Italians. In March 1990, for example, a large gang of Florentine youths battered their way into an immigrant dormitory and beat up immigrant workers. In May 1991, a crowd of Italians cheered as the police arrested a group of Albanians who were demonstrating in the city of Asti to protest the living conditions in their refugee camp. Of all Italians, 75% now favor closing the borders to all new immigration.

The United States has never been a stranger to strangers. Indeed, it would not be much of an exaggeration to characterize America as a nation of immigrants. In 1830, the largest number of our newcomers were Irish; in 1890, they were German. In 1900, they were Italian; then, they were Canadian. During the 1980s, four of five immigrants came from Asia, Latin America, or the Caribbean. By 1990, the newcomers were coming in great numbers from Mexico, the Philippines, Vietnam, China and Taiwan, South Korea, and India. Smaller numbers also entered from the Dominican Republic, El Salvador, Jamaica, and Iran.

The foreign-born population of the United States is currently more than 14 million, by far the largest in the world. Moreover, we are presently in the midst of possibly the largest wave of immigration in U.S. history. Between 1981 and 1990, more than 7 million newcomers, for political as well as economic reasons, pulled up roots and left their homelands to begin new lives in the United States. There will be more newcomers in America in the 1990s than in any previous decade.

In America, as is true elsewhere, the welcome wagon has not always been out for our newcomers, despite their enormous numbers. During the 1982 recession, for example, many Americans held Japanese car manufacturers responsible for massive layoffs in our automobile industry. A 27-year-old Chinese American, Vincent Chin, was spending his Saturday night drinking in a bar located in one of Detroit's working-class neighborhoods. Shouting "It's because of you we're out of work," a Chrysler autoworker and his stepson bludgeoned Chin to death with a baseball bat. From their point of view, *any* Asian was the enemy.

Violence against newcomers also increased during the recession of the early 1990s. In central New Jersey, gangs of white men have driven through local areas populated by Asian Indians, smashing their automobile windshields and shouting anti-Indian slurs. On New Year's Day, 1991, several Indians were assaulted in a diner in the town of Iselin. In May 1991, a young Indian man was hospitalized after being attacked behind a local convenience store.

In May, 1990, three Vietnamese men were assaulted on the streets of Brooklyn, New York. Shouting racial insults, the attackers repeatedly hit one of the victims on the head with a claw hammer. He was hospitalized with a fractured skull.

To some extent, violence directed against newcomers may reflect an almost constant mixture of irrational factors, such as racism, ethnocentrism, and xenophobia. Regardless of the state of the economy at any given point in history, certain members of society—especially those who can trace their own ancestry in a country back several generations—are bound to be offended by, and seek to remove, the strange customs, rituals, and appearance of "inferior outsiders."

At the same time, however, anti-immigrant violence also may have a more practical political and economic basis. First, during periods of economic retrenchment, it sends a powerful message to foreigners from those who seek to reduce competition for jobs. Anti-immigrant violence says to everyone and anyone who might consider emigrating for the sake of a better standard of living: "Your kind is not welcome in *our* country. Don't bother to come. If you do, the same thing will happen to *you*." And to newcomers, it says loud and clear, "Go back where you came from—or else."

As a form of collective scapegoating, violence aimed at newcomers serves a purpose for the rulers of a nation as well. Sociologist Lewis Coser once referred to this phenomenon as a "safety valve." He suggested that when times are bad, hostility that might otherwise be directed at the leaders of a society—its president, prime minister, senators, king, and so on—is instead aimed squarely at its marginal members, those located along the bottommost rungs of the socioeconomic ladder. By focusing blame on the "outsiders," the rulers of a society are able to preserve their positions of power, even if their policies and programs are in fact responsible for pervasive economic hardships.

According to Jorge Bustamante, the president of El Colegio de la Frontera Norte in Tijuana, Mexico, it invariably becomes politically correct to capitalize on anti-immigrant sentiments whenever the United States unemployment rate rises above politically acceptable levels. Politicians then conveniently forget about the role that newcomers play in providing a cheap source of labor that helps keep American industry competitive. They also forget that growing numbers of immigrants spur investments, help revitalize decaying communities, and pay taxes.

When Americans are out of work, we can expect to hear our public officials call for repatriating recent arrivals, establishing more stringent criteria for accepting refugees, and closing the borders with Mexico. This is when immigrants are routinely blamed for Americans being out of work, for trafficking in drugs, for increasing the cost of social services, and for committing violent crime. In 1994, as unemployment rates hovered at 8.5% statewide, Californians passed Proposition 187 in an effort to reduce the cost of providing social services and education to the state's immigrant population.

So what else is new? If there are hard times in America, it must be time to pick on the newcomers! ∎

Race, IQ, and Hysterectomies
Scientists Are Human Beings Too

A study published recently in the *American Journal of Public Health* suggests that a doctor's age and regional location contribute to his odds of doing surgery on women. Specifically, it reports that older gynecologists and doctors living in the South are particularly likely to perform hysterectomies. This may be important information because critics argue that between 25% and 50% of the hundreds of thousands of hysterectomies done every year may be unnecessary, no matter who performs the operation.

If the decision to do surgery were based strictly on the weight of the medical evidence, we would expect age and region to have no effect on hysterectomy rates. This is not the case. In reality, just like everyone else, doctors' medical decisions seem to be based, in part, on where they grew up, what their peers believe to be correct, and what their culture tells them is appropriate. Fad and fashion are as much a part of science as they are of dress designing or popular music. What is stylish in one generation or area of the country may be out of style in another. Objectivity is a scientific goal, but it is not always a reality.

We should keep this in mind when evaluating the heated public debate about race and IQ that has emerged (or reemerged) with the recent publication of *The Bell Curve* by Charles Murray and the late Richard J. Herrnstein. Behavioral scientists once again inform us that the average black American has a lower IQ than the average white American, and that this IQ gap is hereditary.

This is nothing new. In 1969, Arthur Jenson, an educational psychologist, raised the hypothesis that "genetic factors are strongly implicated in the average Negro-White intelligence difference." A survey of the members of the American Psychological Association showed at the time that older psychologists and psychologists living in the South were especially likely to agree with Jenson's thesis.

If agreement with the genetic racial argument were based strictly on the weight of the scientific evidence, we would expect age and region to have no effect on the conclusions that psychologists draw regarding race and IQ. This is not the case. Instead, just like everyone else, psychologists' judgments seem to be based, in part, on where they grew up, what their peers believe to be correct, and what their culture tells them is appropriate. Fad and fashion are as much a part of psychology as they are of dress designing or gynecology.

The argument that minority members are genetically inferior is by no means restricted to black Americans. During the early part of this century, psychologists found that immigrants coming from Poland, Russia, Greece, Turkey, and Italy tended to score lower on intelligence tests than immigrants from northwestern Europe. In support of revising immigration and naturalization laws, psychologists argued in 1923 that newcomers from Southern and Eastern Europe were polluting the stream of intelligence in America. In 1924, based on the testimony of these "objective psychologists," the United States imposed immigration quotas aimed at reducing the flow of "undesirables."

Given the present stage of our knowledge about human behavior, it makes little sense to speculate about racial differences in IQ. First, we must work to wipe out the really important differences that divide us as a people—lack of opportunity, low self-esteem, hopelessness, and despair. We must fight against racism and poverty. Only when these vital differences have been "held constant" will racial differences in intelligence be made clear. In a society in which equality of opportunity is a reality, we won't need scientists to justify our selfishness. ■

"The Economic Escalator" depended a great deal on Kevin Phillips's research in his book *The Politics of the Rich and the Poor* (1990). I also based much of my argument on Katherine Newman's perceptive observations in *Falling From Grace: The Experience of Downward Mobility in the American Middle Class* (1988). As an anthropologist, Newman sees the downwardly mobile as a "very special tribe." She conceives of the experience of generational downward mobility in American society as something "foreign"— as a phenomenon as strange to the members of American society as are the exotic rituals in New Guinea.

Some sociologists believe that social inequality is functional and even necessary to the operation of a society. In an early article, "Some Principles of Stratification," in the *American Sociological Review* (1945), Kingsley Davis and Wilbert Moore argue that at least some degree of social stratification is necessary as a means for rewarding the really important positions in a society. In his highly critical response to Davis and Moore, Melvin Tumin later wrote in his *American Sociological Review* article, "Some Principles of Stratification: A Critical Analysis" (1953), that institutionalized social inequality was also dysfunctional for society. In other words, stratification has some *negative* consequences that were completely ignored by Davis and Moore. Herbert J. Gans takes a modified version of the functional position when he argues in "The Positive Functions of Poverty," in the *American Journal of Sociology* (1972), that the presence of poverty aids in the survival of a society (for example, poor people get the dirty work done, as we saw earlier in the book).

The evidence for "Images of Aging" can be found in a paper titled "Powerful Elders" that I did with Arnold Arluke and William Levin for the 1992 meetings of the American Sociological Association and in *Ageism: Prejudice and Discrimination Against the Elderly* (1980), which Bill Levin and I coauthored. For a summary of the traditional stereotypes associated with older people, see Robert Butler's excellent book, *Why Survive? Being Old in America* (1975). By the way, it was Butler who coined the term *ageism*.

Concerning "The Functions of Immigrant Bashing," I relied a good deal on the numerous journalistic accounts in newspapers and magazines of anti-immigrant episodes around the world. For a particularly comprehensive analysis of the worldwide movement toward immigration and its implications, see the special edition "World Report" section of the *Los Angeles Times* (October 1, 1991). The modern immigrant experience in America is described and analyzed in *Immigrant America: A Portrait* (1990), by Alejandro Portes and Ruben Rumbaut.

Lewis Coser's safety valve idea can be found in his classic work, *The Functions of Social Conflict* (1956). In his enlightening book, *The Rich Get Richer and the Poor Get Prison* (1989), Jeffrey Reiman, based on a conflict approach, presents a criminal justice version of the safety valve function. Reiman attempts to explain why the criminal justice system seems to be preoccupied with dangers usually threatened by violent offenders who are poor. He argues that our attention is diverted from the *real* source of crime, from the injustices of our economic system, and from those rich and powerful members of society who benefit most from the maintenance of the status quo. The dangerous activities of the rich are rarely defined by the legal system as crimes, he says, although such activities result in hundreds of thousands of deaths and the loss of billions of dollars. But the wealthy are weeded out at every stage of the criminal justice system. And in the failure of the criminal justice system, there is a victory for the rich: Hostility is redirected away from the top of the economic order and focused instead on the poor people in our society.

As indicated in "Race, IQ, and Hysterectomies," the claim of a group's being intellectually inferior has been used historically to justify discriminating against its members. *The Bell Curve*, by Charles Murray and the late Richard J. Herrnstein, presents what is merely the newest version of an old theme. For an excellent analysis of how inequality has actually affected the black underclass, read William J. Wilson's *The Truly Disadvantaged* (1987). He argues that the growing problem of permanent poverty among young black men in urban areas can be traced not to any intellectual deficit but to the movement of jobs to the suburbs and to the trend toward a postindustrial economy.

■ DEVELOPING IDEAS *About Social Inequality*

1. Research topic: Make a list of 20 occupations representing the kinds of jobs that you and your classmates are likely to be doing after graduation. Give this list to several friends and ask them to rank all 20 occupations from 1 (most prestigious) to 20 (least prestigious). How much agreement is there regarding the prestige rankings of these jobs? What do your results indicate about the *structured* aspect of stratification?

2. Writing topic: Write a short essay in which you compare the everyday lives of two fictitious characters: a 25-year-old man who possesses extraordinary wealth *versus* a 25-year-old man who experiences extreme poverty. Specifically, compare them on such things as (a) what they are likely to do at leisure, (b) where they are likely to live, (c) their family lives, (d) health care, and (e) their jobs. Explain how each man—the wealthy and the poor—got that way and what the poverty-stricken man might do to improve his social position.

3. Research topic: Popular culture often expresses our stereotyped images. Analyze any 10 birthday cards that you select from your local card shop or drug store. Choose only cards that make a direct reference to age. Are their messages—aside from Happy Birthday—positive or negative? How many refer, if *only* in a joking reference, to lack of sexual activity, lack of attractiveness, lack of intelligence, lack of physical ability? How many joke about age concealment? How many make special mention of *women's* problems with aging? Does any card suggest that you might get better as you get older?

4. Writing topic: Make a list of all the tasks that poor people do for society—tasks that might otherwise not get done or might have to be done by middle-class types. For example, poor people buy day-old bread from thrift stores that might otherwise never be sold. Your turn. By the way, can you also suggest *other ways* to get these tasks accomplished without relying on poor people to do them?

5. Among the methods that sociologists use for assessing social status is the subjective approach whereby the respondents are asked to place themselves in the stratification hierarchy. In 1949, Richard Centers asked a national sample of white adults, "If you were asked to use one of these four names for your

social class, which would you say you belonged in: the middle class, the lower class, working class, or upper class?" Like many other sociologists, Centers found that the majority of his sample saw themselves as belonging to the middle class. Using the same question as Centers, take a sample of 20 people you know fairly well and determine how they see their social class membership—as upper, middle, working, or lower? With which class does the majority identify? Explain your results.

6. Research topic: Every year, the U.S. Bureau of the Census produces a volume, easily accessible at most libraries or through the U.S. Government Printing Office, entitled *Statistical Abstract of the United States*. To determine how inequality may have increased or decreased over time, compare at least two years (say, one year from the 1990s vs. one year from the 1970s) on several indicators of economic well-being, such as unemployment rate, total personal income, families below the poverty level, and average annual pay. You can find these indicators in the table of contents of the book in sections on "Labor Force, Employment, and Earnings" and "Income, Expenditures, and Wealth." You may also decide to look in the section on "Business Enterprise" for business failure rate and employment growth by major industry.

PART SEVEN

Social Change

I've been on a diet for the past 3 months. As of this date, I have lost 24 pounds and hope to lose another 10 or so. Twenty years ago, it would have been relatively easy for me to lose 34 pounds over a short period of time. I would simply have cut down a little on sweets and also reduced the quantity of what I ate at meals. Now that I have reached middle age, however, losing weight seems to require more than just a minor adjustment in my diet. It's not that I lack the will; it's that my metabolism has changed over the years. As a result, only a severe drop in calorie intake along with some kind of exercise regimen seems to make any difference. I really understand, on a "gut" level, why so many Americans suffer from "middle-age spread." If you ask me, the more you age, the more you must reduce your intake of calories to maintain the same weight. Medical research supports my belief.

Just as the structure and functioning of the human body are modified with age, so, too, the structure of our social lives is capable of profound change. In a sense, the "metabolism" of our society changes over time. More and more women have entered the labor force, 25% of all college students are now over 30, and the homicide rate is once again on the rise. It was inconceivable, just a few years ago, that the Berlin Wall would come down or that the Soviet Union would crumble, and yet these changes are now taken-for-granted realities.

By *social change*, then, we refer to modifications in either culture or social structure. Interestingly enough, much social change is orderly. Just as structure has discernible characteristics, so change often has patterns.

Theorists disagree as to precisely what that social change looks like. In the 19th century, theorists such as Herbert Spencer argued that societies inevitably *evolve* from the simple to the complex and always toward greater and greater progress. Karl Marx suggested instead that societies develop through a series of definite stages—from primitive communism, feudalism, capitalism, to socialism—depending on the organization of their economic institutions. Marx believed that all history is the history of class conflict. Finally, some sociologists saw a cyclical pattern in social change. They asserted that history repeats itself. Pitirim Sorokin, for example, identified three cultural themes—ideational, sensate, and idealistic—through which the pendulum of change swings back and forth.

This brief summary of social change theory is meant only to indicate its diversity. Most modern-day sociologists would agree that the earlier theories of social change were too simple. Spencer's views need to be modified: Not all change is for the better; some is for the worse. Progress is far from inevitable. Marx's views need to be modified: Not all conflict is class based. In modern life, we see conflicts between political alliances, age groups, countries, religions, racial groups, and so on. Many of these conflicts generate social change. Sorokin's views need to be modified: The pendulum of change doesn't necessarily swing on the course that he predicted.

Still, the idea of evolution continues to play an important role in our thinking about social change. There seems to be a strong tendency for culture and social structure to become more complex over time. Societies tend to move from small-scale and simple to large-scale and complex forms. Unlike living organisms, however, the evolution cannot be characterized as inevitable. Moreover, the direction and speed of change are not the same in all societies. Societies seem to evolve but on their own terms.

On an individual level, there are literally millions of people who go on diets and take up exercise programs to influence the course of biological change. Many avoid fatty foods, cut down on sugar, or give up red meat. Others buy treadmills and exercise bicycles or jog on a daily basis. Such efforts don't always work as well as we would like. In fact, some dieting plans have an incredibly high 90% failure rate over the long term.

Human beings have similarly sought to help social change along in one or another area of concern. Since 1960, for example, we have seen numerous programs and policies directed toward improving public education; reducing racial, age, and gender discrimination; combating violent crime; improving the economy; and aiding the mentally ill. As suggested in "The Boomerang Effect," not all of these efforts have succeeded as planned. In fact, some of them have only backfired by creating even more social problems for us to solve. The failure rate of programs and policies may not approach 90%, but our effectiveness could be better.

In the 1940s, sociologist Robert Merton recognized that unanticipated and anomalous results—perhaps even the boomerang effect—are rather commonplace in sociological research. Such unexpected, even surprising findings may not always generate the most effective proposals for change at the time, but they frequently have a positive consequence as well. In being forced to deal with inconsistencies and contradictions, sociologists must rethink their work, extend their inadequate theories, or create new theories that better explain the phenomena they seek to understand. In the long run, their *serendipitous* findings may become the basis for more powerful theories of social behavior and more effective social policies and planning.

One thing that I learned the hard way about dieting is that timing is everything. If you're not ready to make the commitment, don't bother trying. If you can't dedicate yourself to an exercise regimen, don't make the effort. You will only fail.

In "Fads: Is Goldfish Gobbling Next?" we observe that popular fads and fashions since the 1920s have depended on the "timing" of changes in the larger culture. Indeed, many fads are made possible by large-scale cultural change. For example, our shared ideas regarding sexuality had been modified so much during the 1960s "sexual revolution" that "streaking" became a widespread activity on college campuses and was usually considered a harmless prank or minor annoyance. Ten years earlier, however, the same act of public nudity would probably have been regarded as a major sexual perversion, and offenders would have been immediately shuffled off to serve long sentences in prison or in a mental hospital.

The aging of the human body is a "mixed bag" of developmental changes. For many people, advanced aging brings about an increase in verbal ability, a more mellow temperament, and more of a tendency to vote. But aging can also engender problems such as a worsening of both memory and hearing.

A major theme in "Riding the Rumor Mill" is that long-standing rumors about crime and disaster in suburban shopping malls actually mirror a trend in the "aging" of our society that many Americans view with alarm. Those social problems once associated with the "inner city" are now spreading to the suburbs, formerly regarded as bastions of middle-class respectability. Suburbanites often express anxiety about maintaining their lifestyle by contributing to unfounded rumors of the demise of the shopping mall. Though focusing on the safety of the mall, they actually express anxiety about more basic changes in their lives.

The human body is a system of interrelated parts. A change in one area has implications for other areas as well. Thus, a healthy diet and sensible exercise program will likely strengthen the functioning of the heart, kidneys, and lungs.

The parts of our society similarly affect one another. "Highway to Hell?" examines the effect of an item of American material culture called the automobile on everyday forms of behavior. Anyone who routinely commutes in rush hour traffic knows the meaning of the term "hot under the collar." Unfortunately, the presence of thousands of pounds of steel in the control of angry and frustrated commuters helps to create the conditions necessary for violent outbursts. Even worse, some motorists who are already angry before they get on the highway decide to go for a drive to "cool off." This creates an explosive mix. Keep in mind, "Highway to Hell?" focuses our attention not on the personality characteristics of drivers but directly on a social situation—the act of driving on our roadways—as it influences differing conceptions of deviant behavior over the decades. But there is another important sociological issue to address: Exactly why did the automobile have such a profound influence on the shape of American cities? And why didn't Americans maximize the use of public transportation?

Its not just the automobile that represents systematic changes over time. Change the structure of the American family (for example, by increasing the number of dual-career families) and you change the economy as well. Change our political institution and you change the character of mass communication. Thus, "Enquiring Times" isn't only about newspapers and books. You don't have to read between the lines to see that celebrity gossip has become an important force in politics and mass entertainment. In the presidential campaign of 1988, for example, Gary Hart was a target; in the more recent election campaign, it was Bill Clinton. Gossip was very much involved in the televised senate hearings to confirm Justice Clarence Thomas and in the televised rape trial of William Kennedy Smith. Millions of Americans "eavesdropped" on an entire cast of characters—Thomas, Hill, Smith—as they divulged the intricate details of their private lives. More recently, O. J. Simpson and the deaths of Nicole Brown Simpson and Ronald Goldman have provided the focal point for small talk during prime time. Some cultures will cut off your lips for gossiping. Here, we just put it on national TV! ∎

The Boomerang Effect in Planning Social Change

In the Social Arena, Good Intentions Sometimes Go Wrong

Usually, social policies and programs are a "mixed bag"; they have multiple effects. We should have learned this lesson from our experience with "hard scientists" who have long recognized the need to weigh costs against benefits in evaluating outcomes. Thalidomide probably eased the suffering of numerous pregnant women; unfortunately, it also produced serious birth deformities. Urea formaldehyde made an extremely effective form of home insulation; it also made some people sick. Antipsychotic drugs improve everyday psychological functioning, but when prescribed without caution, they can also produce an irreversible nervous disorder.

In the social arena, affirmative action legislation has opened doors for women and minorities who would otherwise have been summarily excluded from many decent jobs. It has also stigmatized its beneficiaries by giving the impression that blacks, Latinos, and women enjoy an unfair advantage and are not qualified for the jobs that they hold. Similarly, Social Security is, for many older people, the difference between survival and starvation; it also leads millions of young people to believe that they have no choice but to retire by the age of 65 or 70.

Aside from government intervention, multiple effects often confound those who give the rest of us advice. Marriage counselors who encourage troubled couples to "air their differences" may make their clients feel more comfortable with themselves; they may also inadvertently precipitate a divorce by escalating conflicts between husbands and wives. Nursing homes frequently provide humane care; they also foster dependence. And the voluntary rating system used by the motion picture industry provides guidance in the selection of movies appropriate for children; it also stimulates countless cinematic scenes of gratuitous sex and violence to justify a PG or R rating (the G rating is the kiss of death for the commercial success of a film).

The same principle applies to the influence of the generations. To their credit, people who grew up in the 1960s were deeply involved in the civil rights and women's movements. But they must also take the blame for having weakened our resolve to teach basic skills to our youngsters. The demolition of the open classroom later marked our realization that we were producing a generation of well-adjusted functional illiterates.

In some cases, intelligent people implementing intelligent policies are responsible for producing a "boomerang effect"; they actually create more of whatever it is they seek to reduce in the first place.

The boomerang effect has been achieved many times in recent years by men and women of goodwill. State legislatures around the nation have recently raised the drinking age back to 21 in an effort to reduce the prevalence of violent deaths among our young people. But such policies seem instead to have created the conditions for even more campus violence. Some college students who previously drank in bars and lounges under the watchful supervision of bouncers (not to mention owners eager to keep their liquor licenses) now retreat to the sanctuary of their fraternity houses and apartments, where they no longer control their behavior—or their drinking.

The boomerang effect has also played a role in attempts to reduce the availability of illicit drugs. During recent years, the federal government has been quite successful in reducing the supply of, albeit not the demand for, street drugs such as marijuana. As fields are burned and contraband confiscated, the price of marijuana has skyrocketed to a point where cheap alternatives (for example, "crack") have begun to compete in the marketplace. Unfortunately, the cheap alternatives are even more harmful than the illicit drugs they replace.

Lest those who argue for a "hands-off policy" get too smug, I suggest that the failure to act also has its unanticipated side effects. Ronald Reagan's "benign neglect" in response to poverty in America may have helped cut double-digit inflation; it also reduced the size of the middle class and increased permanent poverty in our cities to an unprecedented level. Moreover, in what was called "deinstitutionalization," we emptied our nation's mental hospitals in the 1970s without providing adequate services or supervision for the mentally ill individuals released into the community. Some of them joined the growing ranks of the homeless; many stopped taking the medications that had made possible their release from institutions.

Of course, not all policies are as well-intentioned as they may appear to be. How do we ascertain another person's motives, let alone those of an organization? Was the ratings system initiated to help parents or to get government off the back of the movie industry? Did all those who supported emptying our mental hospitals really desire more humane treatment of the mentally ill or were they merely trying to cut costs? Even motivation is often a mixed bag.

If a spokesperson for the cigarette industry claims that the link between smoking and lung cancer has not been established, we are suspicious. We may perceive a self-serving, biased assessment. Exactly the same skeptical mind-set is valuable in evaluating the effectiveness of social services and policies—skepticism without cynicism. ■

Fads
Is Goldfish Gobbling Next?

With the all-purpose response "I know, Mom, but everyone's doing it," millions of teenagers have sought to explain to their parents why they experiment with drugs or alcohol, color their hair purple, or wear multiple pierced earrings. Their desire to conform to fashions of their fellows is more than an excuse. Adolescents often do what everyone else is doing—they go along with a fad or fashion simply because they don't want to look different or to be seen as out of step with their peers. Given their other-directedness, teenagers are especially sensitive to what is current versus passé, what is "in" versus "out."

It should come as no surprise, therefore, that many fads and fashions originate in what is called adolescent subculture. By conforming to the latest crazes in haircuts, dress, music, and gadgetry, many teenagers hope to gain approval from their friends.

But peer approval is not the only appeal of such fads. While they hope to impress their friends with their compliance, teenagers also seek to distance themselves from their parents. As a result, behavior that appears to adults to be irrational and even dysfunctional may be valued by the young for exactly that reason: Such behavior is outrageous enough to the older generation. If, when young, their parents drank beer, then the teenagers will try marijuana; if parents wore long hair and peace beads, their offspring will shave their initials into their hair or don spiked jewelry or join the Young Republicans; if parents wore their designer labels under their garments, then their offspring will insist on wearing their labels outside.

Ironically, and of course unwittingly, even the most outrageous teenage fads touchingly reflect the tenor of their times. During the Roaring Twenties, for example, Charles Lindbergh and Amelia Earhart were busy setting records with their derring-do across the Atlantic. Rapid industrial growth and expanding capitalism generated intense competition for scarce economic resources. How did the "flaming youth" of the decade respond? With contests of skill and endurance: flagpole sitting, rocking chair derbies, cross-country races, pea-eating contests, kissing and dancing marathons, gum-chewing and peanut-pushing contests.

During the *Sputnik* era of the late 1950s, competition was once again intense. The United States and the Soviet Union vied for supremacy in science and technology, and American schools responded by attempting to raise their standards. Teenagers once more designed contests to set and break records. Throughout the decade, young people crammed themselves into hearses, Volkswagen Beetles, and telephone booths. They stacked dozens of students on a single bed and stuffed their rooms with papers.

Teenage fashion has also been affected by the culture of its period. During the 1920s, when American women were first allowed to vote, youthful "flappers" literally threw off the bras and corsets of their mother's generation in favor of knee-length skirts, low-cut gowns, and bobbed hair. Some 40 years later, motivated by the women's movement of the 1960s, teenage girls wore miniskirts, cut their hair short, and burned their bras.

Conventional values influence adolescent fads in yet another way. They set the limits as to just how far those fads are permitted to go before adult society enforces sanctions against them. In 1974, undergraduates began to engage in "streaking." To streak was to dash nude through a public place.

Society's tolerance for streaking was a result of the sexual revolution of the 1960s. The same act would undoubtedly have received quite a different reception if it had occurred during the 1950s. Any student who had dared run naked through a college campus then would, in all likelihood, have been quickly locked away as a sexual pervert and a menace to society. In 1954, streaking could hardly have gained the popularity of a fad.

Even the most absurd practices can become the basis for an adolescent fad, given the right social climate. During the Great Depression of the 1930s, at a time when many Americans were having trouble putting food on the table, parents lost their appetites because of a fad that hit college campuses. From Massachusetts to Missouri, students had taken to swallowing goldfish.

A Harvard freshman was the first to swallow a single live fish, while fellow students at the Freshman Union looked on in disgust. Three weeks later, an undergraduate at Franklin and Marshall in Lancaster, Pennsylvania, ate 3 goldfish. New records for goldfish consumption were then set almost daily. At the University of Pennsylvania, one intrepid soul swallowed 25; at the University of Michigan, 28; at Boston College, 29; at Northeastern University, 38; at MIT,

42; and at Clark University, 89 were devoured at one sitting. One college student gained fame by coming up with the first recipe for a goldfish sugar cookie; the chef at the Hotel Statler put the dish on the menu as a special. But a pathologist with the U.S. Public Health Service cautioned that goldfish may contain tapeworms that lodge in the intestines and cause anemia; and by the spring of 1939, the goldfish-gobbling craze had gone the way of the dance marathon.

Teenagers in 1990 tripped over their own feet by wearing their sneakers unlaced; to this day, they continue to increase their susceptibility to illness by refusing to wear winter hats or raincoats and ruin their feet with pointed-toe shoes, all because these are in fashion. In general, they are seen as doing things that aren't very good for them. Teenagers aren't swallowing goldfish yet—but for those who are too young to remember, that could very well be next. ■

Riding the Rumor Mill
Our Basic Anxieties Are Projected in Various Tall Tales

Rumors frequently touch on our important fears and anxieties. Where food shortages exist, individuals circulate stories about the supply and distribution of provisions; where access to economic resources depends on tracing descent through uncertain genealogies, they gossip about one another's ancestors; where witchcraft is a cultural belief, they spread tales about who is and is not a witch; and when economic times are bad, workers depend on the office grapevine to forecast management changes.

Temple University's Ralph Rosnow suggests that rumors on a national level prey on our basic anxieties about death, disaster, and illness. Thus, a number of celebrities have reportedly died in the face of overwhelming evidence to the contrary (including their personal denials)—Paul McCartney, Jerry Mathers of *Leave It to Beaver* fame, and Life Cereal's "Mikey," to mention a few. Some who have, by all credible accounts, actually died—Elvis, Jim Morrison, JFK, and Hitler—have been seen alive! In addition, many recent rumors have incorrectly reported the contamination of popular food; for example, spider eggs in bubble gum, candy that explodes when eaten with a carbonated beverage, worms in hamburgers, mice in Coke bottles, rats in fried chicken, and cats in Chinese food.

According to Tulane sociologist Fredrick Koenig, author of *Rumor in the Marketplace: The Social Psychology of Commercial Hearsay,* rumors do not necessarily reduce anxiety; instead, they often confirm our worst suspicions. But in one sense, such doomsday stories can also be comforting; for at the very least, they confirm the validity of our perception of the world, especially if we see that world as dangerous.

The anxiety multiplies when the "danger" is seen as encroaching on our personal safety. Take living in the suburbs, for example. For decades, young families scrimped and sacrificed, denying themselves all but the barest necessities to accumulate the down payment on their "dream house" in East Norwich, New York; Longmeadow, Massachusetts; or Glencoe, Illinois. By moving to the suburbs, they had hoped to escape the poverty, crime, and congestion associated with city living.

But during the past decade, the suburban version of the American Dream slipped away, as real estate values and property taxes skyrocketed, the quality of local services declined, pollution increased, energy costs remained high, and crime invaded the outer reaches of suburbia. On a daily basis, local newspapers reported increasing incidents of the very crimes that anxious suburbanites had left the city to escape—forcible rape, aggravated assault, and automobile theft. Facing severe tax restrictions at the local level, suburban school systems began laying off teachers, firemen, and police. Public roads and buildings were left in a state of disrepair. And in the process, the suburbs increasingly began to resemble the pathologies associated with urban decay.

In 1979, tension surrounding an "invader" of the suburbs—the Reverend Sun Myung Moon's Unification Church, the so-called Moonies, which purchased real estate in Gloucester, Massachusetts—manifested in a "classic" rumor. Hearing stories of teenagers coerced into the Moonie cause, people began believing that the regionally powerful Entenmann's Bakery was owned by the Unification Church and that its products were tainted.

Although Entenmann's was then actually owned by the Warner-Lambert Corporation, that detail didn't stop hundreds of customers from complaining to store managers who carried Entenmann's products. Moreover, church bulletins, letters to the editor, and callers to radio talk shows all warned about Moonie ownership of the bakery and urged everyone to boycott Entenmann's products. As they attempted to deliver their goods, Entenmann's drivers were physically assaulted by angry customers. The bakery's sales declined. So long as public anxiety remained at a high level, Entenmann's continued to serve as a convenient, albeit innocent, target of hostility.

Eventually, the anxieties fueling the Entenmann's rumors faded into the distance. In its place, rumormongering about the deterioration of suburbia coalesced around images of the shopping mall as dangerous and threatening, as a place where the most pernicious influences of the inner city had altered suburban life. After all, the mall had previously represented the heart and soul of the suburban lifestyle, being inaccessible except by automobile, protected from crime by security guards, sheltered by its physical isolation, and attractive to a largely homogeneous segment of the middle-class customers who spent their days leisurely strolling through the corridors spending money. If crime and poverty invaded the tranquil, secure confines of the suburban shopping mall, then absolutely nobody was safe.

In 1983, in western Massachusetts, there surfaced a story about a "woman" shopping at a local mall who asked various customers for a ride home. It was said that when authorities finally apprehended her, she turned out to be an axe-wielding man wearing makeup and a wig to protect his true identity. Similarly in the early 1980s, Connecticut residents picked up various stories about a young girl who suddenly disappeared while walking with her mother in a mall. According to this tale, worried security guards later found her in a restroom, where she had been given a short haircut and dressed in boy's clothing. By 1985, some version of these mall stories had spread all over the country from New York to Texas to California. Only the name of the shopping center and some of the details of the "crime" varied from location to location.

The rumors of abduction and crime in suburban shopping malls, although not completely gone, have receded somewhat. But in their place, there are new reports around the country that newly constructed shopping malls are in imminent danger of being transformed into underground shopping centers; they are, it is said, structurally unsound and literally sinking.

In the most recent episode, the mammoth, three-story Emerald Square Mall in North Attleboro, Massachusetts, has been the target of unfounded rumors since it opened in August 1989. Among the most widely told tales are those that contend that the mall has already sunk 6 inches, that its third floor has been closed, that the top floor of the adjoining parking garage has been closed, that the garage has separated from the main building, that many of the windows have shattered, that the mall will soon close, and that the mall will be torn down and rebuilt. Although there is no truth in any of this, that hasn't prevented customers from phoning the mall's building inspector with wild stories, excitedly discussing the rumors in shops and restaurants, and, in some cases, taking their business elsewhere.

Those who attempt to explain such rumors of sinking shopping malls might point to some offhand, ill-informed remark made by an engineer or the presence of a neighboring shopping center that really did have structural problems. People sometimes do get confused by the facts. But for those who take a long-term view, the sinking-mall rumors are merely a new variation of an old theme, beginning with the stories of children allegedly being abducted from mall restrooms and continuing with the axe-wielding "woman." You don't have to be Freud to figure it out: It really isn't the shopping mall sinking we worry about—it is our whole way of life. ∎

Highway to Hell?
Fear and Loathing on the Road

Travel any highway into a major city during rush hour. While waiting to move, you are bound to observe at least a half dozen drivers talking to themselves, singing along with a tune on the radio, or scratching themselves.

Automobiles give an *illusion* of privacy. So long as drivers remain behind the wheel, they travel in isolation. Enclosed by steel and glass, they are physically independent of the thousands of other motorists with whom they share the road. No matter how jammed the highway is with vehicles, drivers feel alone, and in a social-psychological sense, they are. As a result, they may engage in bizarre, even deviant, behavior.

Having been associated with deviance ever since the advent of mass motoring, automobiles have long contributed to the direction of social and cultural change. In the 1920s, many Americans for the first time owned a family car. And it was the automobile that critics blamed for what they saw as a precipitous decline in national morality. Newly freed from the rigid restrictions of previous generations, the "flaming youth" of the decade regarded the family's "tin lizzie" as their "apartment on wheels"—a place where they could kiss, neck, and pet. Sex researcher Alfred Kinsey reported that young women of the 1920s were far more likely to have premarital intercourse than were those who had reached sexual maturity before World War I. Not surprisingly, the automobile was blamed—and with cause. In Robert and Helen Lynd's 1929 classic community study, *Middletown*, the overwhelming majority of teenagers in Muncie, Indiana, reported that the automobile was the most common place to pet.

In a more extreme version of immorality, the automobile of the 1920s also became a "brothel on wheels," providing ladies of the night from red light districts around the country a secure and secluded place where they might escape police oversight and ply their trade. The use of the automobile for purposes of prostitution posed a serious setback to the vigorous antivice campaigns of the World War I period. The police were not yet equipped to patrol city streets and country highways.

By the 1950s, teenagers around the country were holding their "submarine races" in lovers' lanes and drive-in theaters. The game of "chicken" became a deadly contest between males who sought to impress their dates. During subsequent decades, young people relied on their automobiles as a safe haven in which to drink beer, have sex, and smoke dope.

Teenagers aren't the only drivers who play chicken. Every year, some 46,000 Americans—from all age groups—are killed in motor vehicle accidents. Another 1.8 million are disabled. Among the leading causes of such fatal crashes are drinking and speeding—two human factors that could be totally controlled. In some single-victim automobile "accidents," the lack of control is deliberate: The driver purposely veers into a tree or off a bridge to commit suicide. These victims choose an automobile as an instrument for taking their own lives to save their families the embarrassment that accompanies more obvious forms of suicide.

But most deaths and injuries are avoidable. Such accidents happen because the automobile offers power—especially to the powerless. The automobile is a vehicle that satisfies the desire to be in charge. Even the most timid and passive individuals (or perhaps *especially* the most timid and passive individuals) may become fearless bullies and criminals as soon as they get behind the 3,000 pounds of steel that separate them from the rest of humanity. Not only do they feel anonymous; they also feel invulnerable—caught up in an *illusion* of their own omnipotence.

At the extreme, unbridled power turns nasty, and arguments between drivers erupt into violence. The freeways of California have been particularly violent for the past decade, as small provocations send some frustrated motorists into a state of frenzy. In Sacramento, a passenger inflamed by a freeway lane change lifted a rifle from a rack in the back window of his pickup truck and fatally shot the driver of the other vehicle. One passenger was shot in the head after a minor sideswiping incident. A tow truck operator was fired on by a driver who had blocked his entry onto the Golden State Freeway. In Claremont, the windshields of 10 vehicles were smashed and a police officer was fired on as he prepared to write a traffic ticket. During a single 2-week period (August 1987) there were 18 different acts of violence on the highways of the Silicon Valley, not to mention the rest of California. What is more, shooting episodes quickly spread across the country to trigger-happy drivers in Detroit, Boston, and New York.

For commuters, the experience of driving in rush hour traffic is intensely frustrating. In most major cities, parking places have become as rare as pollution-free air; and traffic jams at 5 p.m. are beginning to resemble never-ending parking lots. For visitors, the problems associated with negotiating traffic are exacerbated by a lack of street signs and the presence of one-way streets without pattern or logic.

Some drivers are already frustrated before they get behind the wheel of their vehicles. They decide to go for a drive to "cool off" after arguing with their boss, their spouse, or their friends. According to University of California psychologist Joseph Tupin, people with aggressive impulses frequently take their cars out for a spin as a release from the tensions of the day. They get into a minor confrontation on the highway and explode.

Of course, the most pervasive effects of the automobile are at the level of social change. As we have seen, the presence of the family car, beginning in the 1920s, significantly altered the ability of young people to achieve independence from their families. At the same time, the opportunities for deviant behavior became much more difficult to challenge. Moreover, the pattern of commuting traffic in most major cities has determined, for the most part, the clustering of skyscrapers, the placement of sports arenas and convention centers, work schedules, the direction of suburban sprawl, and the aesthetics of urban life generally. In a few cities (for example, Los Angeles), the urban landscape is virtually dominated by the presence of interconnected networks of freeways.

Americans continue their love affair with their cars. No matter how efficient, public transportation will probably never quite take the place of the beloved automobile. After all, the gargantuan automobile industry (not to mention all of the peripheral industries that it has spawned) literally cannot afford for that to happen and so continues to spend incredibly large amounts of money for advertisements and commercials in which the virtues of driving are extolled. It is perhaps no exaggeration to suggest that the automobile is now as American as apple pie. Of course, so is violence. ∎

Enquiring Times

The Tabloidization of Hard News

I confess to having thumbed through a copy or two of the *National Enquirer* and the *Star*, usually while waiting in line at the supermarket checkout counter. It takes little more than a cursory reading to discover that the "two-headed baby" stories—the gory items for which they are notorious—have all but disappeared. According to a recent article in *Journalism Quarterly*, the tabloids now print profiles; 61% of their articles focus on celebrities (singer Michael Jackson's obsession with cleanliness, Dolly Parton's diet, Johnny Carson's latest divorce) and 37% on the accomplishments of ordinary people who do extraordinary things (the man who lost 350 pounds by stapling his stomach, the 87-year-old woman who gave up her Social Security check to feed the homeless, the man who swam for 4 days in shark-infested waters).

For those who prefer the gore, there are still a few, relatively obscure tabloids that specialize in it. The *Sun* and the *Weekly World News* can be counted on for a story featuring a "human pregnant with animal" or an "animal pregnant with human." But the most popular supermarket tabloids—the *National Enquirer*, the *Star*, the *Globe*, and the *National Examiner*—have removed most of the grisly pieces, and they still attract some 10 million readers.

These tabloids continue to run into thorny ethical problems, however, mainly concerning their aggressive methods of reporting and their reliance on hearsay rather than "hard news." Hollywood celebrities often claim that *Enquirer* reporters invade their privacy, rely on unreliable informants, and fabricate information about their personal lives. As a result, tabloids continue to have only marginal status among print journalists.

Yet mainstream journalists must be aware, perhaps even envious, of the tremendous popularity of supermarket tabloids. At a time when newspapers around the country are shutting down, publishers are looking for new models that might keep them in business.

Because of their vast appeal, the supermarket tabloids have provided such a model. Many mainstream papers have become *tabloidized;* that is, they have imitated not only the tabloid's size and shape but its sensational headlines. Some have begun to rely more on hearsay and ethically questionable investigative techniques. The *National Enquirer* continues to be the butt of criticism from Hollywood celebrity types, television talk show hosts, and the public. It remains a whipping boy of mainstream journalists, even as they imitate its content and format.

Before we blame the messenger for sending a message we detest, let us recognize that the tabloidization of news reflects a large-scale social change: Gossip about powerful people has assumed an important place in the American psyche. During the 1960s, we treated our rich and famous like royalty. They could do no wrong; and if they did, we would look the other way. John F. Kennedy's acts of infidelity in the White House were summarily ignored by the press. Whatever their faults and frailties, the rich and powerful were still regarded as paragons of virtue and exemplars for the ethical and intellectual standards we hoped to impart to our children.

In the wake of Watergate, Chappaquiddick, Abscam, Irangate, Jim and Tammy Bakker, Leona Helmsley, Ivan Boesky, Whitewater, Bob Packwood, and the savings and loan scandal, however, public naïveté gave way to widespread skepticism, if not outright cynicism. We could no longer trust the people who ran things—the national politicians, Hollywood celebrities, and New York business tycoons. They were caught too often literally with their pants down.

In response to an apparently insatiable appetite for gossip, information about the private lives of public figures has become a mainstay of front-page news, just as it has long been the backbone of tabloid journalism. It was not the *Star* or the *National Examiner* but the legitimate *Las Vegas Sun* that first revealed that Liberace was dying of AIDS. It was not the *National Examiner* but the *Miami Herald* that snooped on Gary Hart to expose his affair with Donna Rice. Gossip about the lives of such celebrities as Bill Clinton, Kitty Dukakis, Nancy Reagan, Barney Frank, Ted Kennedy, Martin Luther King, Jr., and Gerry Studds has been featured in front-page stories, not only in the *Star* but in local newspapers around the country.

Some people still remember Carol Burnett's successful mid-1970s lawsuit against the *National Enquirer*. She was able to show that the tabloid had acted with reckless disregard for the truth when it published defamatory information about her. According to University of Arkansas Law Professor Rodney Smolla, the establishment press tried, in the wake of a verdict favorable to Burnett, to disassociate itself from such tabloids as the *Enquirer*.

Tabloid journalism uses hearsay—the anonymous source—as a method for collecting information about celebrities' private lives. Establishment newspapers are known for their reliance on eyewitness accounts and interviews with participants. But legitimate print and broadcast journalists have made mistakes of their own, some of which rival, if not surpass, the *Enquirer*'s shoddy treatment of Burnett. Increasingly, libel cases have been successfully aimed at mainstream news ranging from *60 Minutes* to *Time* magazine.

Northeastern University sociologist Arnold Arluke and I tried to determine the prevalence of hearsay in legitimate front-page journalism. To this end, we examined the front page of the *New York Times* Sunday edition from October 1985 to September 1986. We found that as many as 70% of these front-page stories were unattributable. Many were so vague that they could have referred to almost anyone: "sources close to the investigation," "officials," "intelligence sources," "a key official," "critics," "campaign strategists," and the like. Some reporters even admitted to using thirdhand sources or obtaining information over the phone from an unknown person.

The reliable source has always been an important and legitimate technique of investigative journalism. (Without "Deep Throat," we might never have learned of the Watergate cover-up.) In the 1970s, unadulterated hearsay could be found in only 35% of the front-page articles published in the *New York Times*. But in the 1990s, the anonymous source has become common in front-page reportage.

When *Enquirer* reporters use an anonymous source to get some "dirt" on Carol Burnett, they harm one individual. When a daily newspaper uncritically accepts the word of an anonymous source concerning an international event, it may damage the reputation of an entire country or the relationship between nations. When the *Star* bases a story about Michael Jackson on "a source close to the celebrity," we are skeptical. When the *New York Times* or the *Washington Post* relies on an off-the-record comment to develop a front-page story, we think of it as hard news. In the era of the tabloidization of news, the distinction between supermarket tabloids and legitimate daily newspapers has blurred in fact, if not yet in the public mind. ■

Which came first—the chicken or the egg? In sociology, the debate is frequently between religion and the economy. For a classic account of the influence of Protestantism on capitalism, read Max Weber's *The Protestant Ethic and the Spirit of Capitalism* (1958). To examine the opposite view—that the state of the economy determines the direction of the religious institution—read Karl Marx and Frederick Engels's *On Religion* (1964).

As discussed in "The Boomerang Effect in Planning Social Change," even the best intentions sometimes go awry. Robert Merton's essay concerning unanticipated findings is found in *Social Theory and Social Structure* (1957). For a more recent discussion of the boomerang effect, read Samuel Sieber's book *Fatal Remedies* (1981).

Concerning "Fads," I owe much of my analysis to Ernie Anastos's *Twixt: Teens Yesterday and Today* (1983). He provides an engrossing photo history of changing adolescent fashion, hairstyles, dances, and heroes since the 1920s. For a discussion of fashion as it relates to gender roles and aging, I also recommend Alison Lurie's readable, intriguing, and often sociological book, *The Language of Clothing* (1981). *American Fads* (1985), by Richard Johnson, provides a description of 40 fads, from silly putty and swallowing goldfish to hot pants and Hula Hoops.

My discussion of changing shopping mall rumors in "Riding the Rumor Mill" was based in large part on ideas developed by psychologists and sociologists over a span of 50 years. I gathered the details of particular rumors by talking with the reporters who covered the stories and by reading their newspaper accounts. Psychologists have long defined rumor as a message passed by word of mouth that becomes increasingly distorted as it travels from person to person. See Gordon Allport and Leo Postman's "The Basic Psychology of Rumor," in *Readings in Social Psychology*, edited by G. E. Swanson, T. M. Newcomb, and E. L. Hartley (1952). From a sociological point of view, however, rumor can be regarded as an informal source of news, a collective experience that the members of a group employ to define an extraordinary situation. After an earthquake hits an area, for example, you can count on the spread of rumor to fill gaps in public anxiety—until official information is finally available. This sociological conception can be found in

Tamotsu Shibutani's pioneering work titled *Improvised News* (1966). The link between anxiety and rumormongering was made clear in Ralph Rosnow and Gary Fine's excellent book, *Rumor and Gossip: The Social Psychology of Hearsay* (1976). For an insightful account of the spread of commercial rumors, read Fredrick Koenig's *Rumor in the Marketplace: The Social Psychology of Commercial Hearsay* (1985).

"Highway to Hell?" focuses attention on the impact of technology (in this case, the automobile) in determining the direction and quality of social change. Many theorists have emphasized the role of technological innovation, beginning with William Ogburn's (1950) classic treatment titled *Social Change*, which he originally published in 1922. To illustrate the power of technology in the process of social change, Ogburn suggested that slavery in the United States was greatly encouraged by the invention of the cotton gin in 1795. By increasing productivity and therefore profits, this single technological innovation—the gin—depended on large numbers of laborers to work the cotton fields. The plantation economy quickly dominated the southern landscape, where it remained in full force for more than a hundred years.

Concerning "Enquiring Times," much of the research was taken from my work with Arnold Arluke as reported in *Gossip: The Inside Scoop* (1987). For this book, we interviewed gossip columnists and tabloid reporters and studied supermarket tabloids, popular celebrity biographies, and the front page of the *New York Times*. For an excellent treatment of the role of gossip as an agent of social control cross-culturally, try Sally E. Merry's chapter, "Rethinking Gossip and Scandal," in *Toward a General Theory of Social Control*, edited by Donald Black (1984).

■ DEVELOPING IDEAS *About Social Change*

1. Research topic: This task requires some library work. Find a best-selling magazine that has been around for several decades and contains advertisement photos featuring men and women. Take at least a couple of different time periods—for example, war versus peace time, prosperity versus recession. Examine each ad photo to determine how changes in the larger society

may have influenced fashions of the day. Be sure to keep a written record of important information, such as the year, magazine title, whether the model in an ad was a man or a woman, and so on.

2. Research topic: Do a kind of sociological "family tree" that might inform you about social changes over the generations. For example, go back in your own family at least two generations, comparing yourself with their parents and your grandparents. Compare the generations on variables such as (a) last year of school completed, (b) jobs held, (c) place of birth, (d) favorite music, (e) the racial composition of neighbors on the block while growing up, (f) attitudes toward family life, and (g) cost of a single-family home or monthly rent.

3. Writing topic: After conducting research in Exercise 2 above, write a short essay in which you discuss social changes over three generations, using your own family to illustrate.

4. Research topic: This is a project to determine changes in the importance of gossip in election campaigns. Go to the library and locate files of a daily newspaper that has been around for a few decades. Compare the front-page newspaper coverage of any presidential election campaign before 1970 versus the coverage of the 1992 campaign. You might want to limit yourself to reading the front-page of Sunday papers beginning with the Iowa caucus or the New Hampshire primary and ending with election day. How many references do you find concerning the personal lives of the candidates? How many references do you find regarding their moral character? How have the "issues" changed?

5. Writing topic: The role of the automobile—as an item of material culture—in social change has been discussed. Unlike Canada and many European countries, America never developed its system of public transportation to its maximum potential. In a short essay, develop the argument, begun in the essay, that the automobile industry is largely responsible for maintaining our love affair (or should I say marriage) with the automobile, to the exclusion of alternatives such as public buses, trains, and subways.

INTO THE FUTURE

One of the most important goals of sociology as a social science is to make accurate predictions. As far as the major problems of American society are concerned, William J. Wilson's *The Truly Disadvantaged* (1987) has focused squarely on the state of the black underclass. If Wilson is correct, the ranks of the permanently unemployed may continue to swell. Not that the future of poverty in America wasn't at least vaguely discernible decades ago. Daniel Bell, in 1973, was already speculating about the characteristics of postindustrial America in his book, *The Coming of the Postindustrial Society: A Venture in Social Forecasting.*

In *Forecasting Crime Data* (1978), my colleague James A. Fox provides an important example of the way in which sociologists can successfully make projections into the future based on demographic data. He correctly predicted the soaring crime rate we are presently experiencing. Unfortunately, he sees more of the same in the years ahead.

But sociologists aren't psychics; we don't pretend to have perfectly clear snapshots of the future (we are doing well to come up with clear pictures of the present). Like economists and political scientists, we may be willing occasionally to take an educated guess as to the direction of society, admitting that there are too many variables to make precise predictions about almost anything. Sure, X will grow, unless, of course, Y suddenly declines. Sure, A will improve, assuming, of course, B isn't modified first. We don't always know Y and B, so our projections about X and A are less than perfect. And we haven't even mentioned the assumptions we make about $C, D, E, F, G, H, I, J, K, L, M, N, O, P, Q, R, S, T, U, V, W,$ and Z—the many other important variables that influence changes in social structure and culture.

It's not just sociologists, of course, who are imperfect prognosticators. Few economists were able to predict the energy shortage that began in 1973; even fewer political scientists forecast the crumbling of the Berlin Wall or the toppling of the Soviet Union. And our 1991 Persian Gulf war seemed to come out of nowhere, as far as the literature of social science is concerned.

By the year 2000, the leading edge of the baby boom generation will be well into its late fifties, and their children will be approaching young adulthood. Like every other generation, the baby boomers will make plans to retire from the labor force. However, they won't feel pressured to do so. Instead, they are likely to be offered incentives to *remain* in what is likely to become an ever-shrinking labor force. At this point, you can expect the typical retirement age to move from 65 to 70, or even older. Early retirement will all but disappear as an option.

Also by the turn of the century, the children of the baby boomers will be deeply entrenched in the crime-prone age group—late teens through early 20s (there will be a 23% increase in the number of teenagers over the next decade), and the rate of violent crime is likely to soar, even by today's horrific standards. For the same reason, college admissions requirements are likely to become increasingly competitive. Academically marginal and older students (those often called "nontraditional" by college administrators) will have to compete against growing numbers of traditionally defined "college-aged" students—children of the baby boomers between the ages of 18 and 22. Academic "late-bloomers" are likely to lose out, as they are no longer wooed by formerly eager admissions committees.

If they are like every generation to precede them, the aging baby boomers will reduce their spending and stop using credit cards. As they actually begin to retire from the labor force, the boomers will, as a result, finally forfeit their cultural clout as well. Just as members of the "twentysomething" generation presently feels it is playing second fiddle to the boomers, so more and more young Americans in the future will resent the presence of huge · numbers of retired Gruppies (gray urban professionals) who live on their Social Security checks and require expensive health care insurance to survive.

By the year 2000, multiculturalism will become a focal point of social change. Growing numbers of immigrants and minorities—African, Asian, and Latin Americans—will ensure that the white Anglo-Saxon majority is no longer the majority. In our postindustrial society, there will be growing conflict between groups for scarce economic resources.

In their recent effort, *The Good Society* (1991), Robert Bellah, Richard Madsen, William Sullivan, Ann Swidler, and Steven Tipton argue that we can solve our growing social problems by transforming our institutions—our schools, family, corporations, church, and state. As they so eloquently did in *Habits of the Heart* (1985), Bellah et al. decry the rise of raw individualism in American society. Calling for public debate concerning our social ills, they propose a blueprint for the future of American society. In *The Good Society*, they assert that we are fully capable of making changes in our values and of taking responsibility for our economic and political institutions. The technological outlook may be even rosier, according to Gene Bylinski. In an article in *Fortune* titled "Technology in the Year 2000" (1988), he is sanguine regarding our ability to employ future technological discoveries to heal the human body and help us to live fuller lives.

Sociology has often been regarded as subversive. In a sense, it is. That is to say, sociologists often challenge our taken-for-granted assumptions, the status quo, and, more precisely, the people in charge of things. No wonder totalitarian societies rarely permit their college students to study the field of sociology; or when they do, they keep it under rigid controls. For the same reason, even in societies that permit greater freedom of choice, sociologists aren't always welcome or appreciated. They might rock the political boat. They might advocate expensive programs and policies. Their research might be useful to reformists who agitate for social change.

The importance of the field of sociology—or more precisely, the collective respect for it—varies according to the urgency of our social problems and the extent of our prosperity as a society. In popular culture terms, we have to believe that we *need* sociologists, but we also have to feel we can *afford* them. The "hip generation" of the 1960s and early 1970s, for example, was a heyday for the field. By 1973, the number of college students earning their bachelor's degrees in sociology had reached a record high of 35,996. Inflation was relatively low, the economy was growing, and there were several important social issues to inspire interest. Civil rights, feminism, and war were on almost everybody's mind. Our inner cities were burning, while thousands marched through the streets to protest, demonstrate, or riot. As a result, millions looked to social scientists to give them advice about how to run society, how to solve the urgent problems of the day. Not that anyone in charge often implemented the answers that sociologists provided, but at least we were asked.

In the February 3, 1992, issue of *Newsweek*, reporter Barbara Kantrowitz, in her article "Sociology's Lonely Crowd," summarizes some of the problems and prospects of the discipline. She reports that by 1989, the number of students receiving bachelor's degrees in sociology had dwindled to only 14,393. Long holding a reputation as being among the more liberal of the arts and sciences, sociology apparently did not fit very well into the cultural milieu of the 1980s. Students turned to majors such as business and engineering—majors they considered to be more "practical." Moreover, many undergraduates enrolled in specialized professional programs—criminal justice, social work, urban studies, and market research—which began in and are actually offshoots of sociology.

In the last few years, however, we have seen a reversal of this trend. Enrollment in sociology courses is again on the rise. We are just beginning to recognize the need to address growing social problems such as homelessness, crime, and poverty. The black underclass is perhaps four times larger today than it was in the 1960s when civil disorder enveloped our major cities in flames. Kids are murdering one another at ever-younger ages. If present trends continue unabated, it is safe to predict that sociologists will gain prominence into the next century. The United States continues to struggle with long-standing problems that reduce our quality of life and frustrate our collective aspirations. Finding effective solutions will require that we put aside our differences and pull together as a society. We can only hope that Americans will rise to the challenge.

Bibliography

Allport, Gordon, & Postman, Leo (1952). The basic psychology of rumor. In G. E. Swanson, T. M. Newcomb, & E. L. Hartley (Eds.), *Readings in social psychology*. New York: Holt.

Anastos, Ernie (1983). *Twixt: Teens yesterday and today*. New York: Franklin Watts.

Archer, Dane, & Gartner, Rosemary (1984). *Violence and crime in cross-national perspective*. New Haven, CT: Yale University Press.

Arms, Robert, & Goldstein, Jeffrey (1979). Effects of viewing aggressive sports on the hostility of spectators. *Social Psychology Quarterly, 42,* 275-279.

Asch, Solomon (1952). Effects of group pressure upon the modification and distortion of judgment. In G. E. Swanson (Ed.), *Readings in social psychology*. New York: Rinehart & Winston.

Ball-Rokeach, Sandra, & Cantor, Muriel (1986). *Media, audience, and social structure*. Beverly Hills, CA: Sage.

Barcus, F. Earle (1983). *Images of life on children's television: Sex roles, minorities, and families*. New York: Praeger.

Bateson, Mary Catherine (1990). *Composing a life*. New York: Plume.

Becker, Howard S. (1967). Whose side are we on? *Social Problems, 14,* 239-247.

Becker, Howard S., Greer, Blanche, Hughes, Everett C., & Strauss, Amselm L. (1961). *Boys in white*. Chicago: University of Chicago Press.

Bell, Daniel (1973). *The coming of the postindustrial society: A venture in social forecasting*. New York: Basic Books.

Bellah, Robert, Madsen, Richard, Sullivan, William, Swidler, Ann, & Tipton, Steven (1985). *Habits of the heart: Individualism and commitment in American life*. Berkeley: University of California Press.

Bellah, Robert, Madsen, Richard, Sullivan, William, Swidler, Ann, & Tipton, Steven (1991). *The good society*. New York: Knopf.

Bowers, William J. (1974). *Executions in America*. Lexington, MA: Lexington Books.

Breines, Winifred (1992). *Young, white, and miserable: Growing up female in the fifties*. Boston: Beacon.

Butler, Robert (1975). *Why survive? Being old in America*. New York: Harper & Row.

Bylinski, Gene (1988, July 18). Technology in the year 2000. *Fortune*.

Cantor, Muriel, & Pingree, Suzanne (1983). *The soap opera*. Beverly Hills, CA: Sage.

Chernin, Kim (1981). *The obsession: Reflections on the tyranny of slenderness*. New York: Harper & Row.

Chudacoff, Howard (1989). *How old are you?* Princeton, NJ: Princeton University Press.

Cooley, Charles H. (1902). *Human nature and the social order*. New York: Scribner.

Comstock, Gary D. (1991). *Violence against lesbians and gay men*. New York: Columbia University Press.

Coser, Lewis (1956). *The functions of social conflict*. New York: Free Press.

Davis, Kingsley, & Moore, Wilbert (1945). Some principles of stratification. *American Sociological Review, 10*, 242-249.

Donnerstein, Edward, Linz, Daniel, & Penrod, Steven (1987). *The question of pornography*. New York: Free Press.

Durkheim, Émile (1933). *The division of labor in society*. New York: Free Press.

Durkheim, Émile (1951). *Suicide: A study in sociology*. New York: Free Press.

Durkheim, Émile (1966). *The rules of sociological method*. New York: Free Press.

Ehrlich, Howard J. (1990). *Campus ethnoviolence and the policy options*. Baltimore, MD: National Institute Against Prejudice and Violence.

Erikson, Eric H. (1950). *Childhood and society*. New York: Norton.

Faludi, Susan (1991). *Backlash: The undeclared war against American women.* New York: Crown.

Fox, James A. (1978). *Forecasting crime data.* Lexington, MA: Lexington Books.

Fox, James A., & Levin, Jack (1994). *Overkill: Mass murder and serial killing exposed.* New York: Plenum.

Gans, Herbert J. (1972). The positive functions of poverty. *American Journal of Sociology, 78,* 275-289.

Gerbner, George, Gross, Larry, Morgan, Michael, & Signorielli, Nancy (1982). Charting the mainstream: Television's contributions to political orientations. *Journal of Communication, 32,* 100-127.

Gerth, H. H., & Mills, C. Wright (Eds.). (1946). *Max Weber: Essays in sociology.* New York: Oxford University Press.

Glazer, Myron Peretz, & Glazer, Penina Migdal (1989). *The whistleblowers: Exposing corruption in government and industry.* New York: Basic Books.

Goffman, Erving (1958). *Asylums.* New York: Anchor.

Goffman, Erving (1963). *Stigma: Notes on the management of spoiled identity.* Englewood Cliffs, NJ: Prentice Hall.

Goldstein, Jeffrey (1986). *Aggression and crimes of violence* (2nd ed.). New York: Oxford University Press.

Gottfredson, Michael, & Hirschi, Travis (1990). *A general theory of crime.* Stanford, CA: Stanford University Press.

Granfield, Robert (1986). Legal education as corporate ideology. *Sociological Forum, 1,* 514-523.

Harris, Marvin (1979). *Cultural materialism.* New York: Random House.

Herek, Gregory, & Berrill, Kevin (Eds.). (1992). *Hate crimes: Confronting violence against lesbians and gay men.* Newbury Park, CA: Sage.

Hughes, Everett (1962). Good people and dirty work. *Social Problems, 10,* 3-11.

Johnson, Richard (1985). *American fads.* New York: Beech Tree.

Jones, Landon Y. (1980). *Great expectations: America and the baby boom generation.* New York: Ballantine.

Kalberg, Stephen (1980). Max Weber's types of rationality: Cornerstones for the analysis of rationalization processes in history. *American Journal of Sociology, 85,* 1145-1179.

Kanter, Rosabeth M. (1993). *Men and women of the corporation* (2nd ed.) New York: Basic Books.

Kantrowitz, Barbara (1992, February 3). Sociology's lonely crowd. *Newsweek.*

Katz, Jack (1988). *Seductions of crime: Moral and sensual attractions of doing evil.* New York: Basic Books.

Kaufman, Debra Renee (1991). *Rachel's daughters.* New Brunswick, NJ: Rutgers University Press.

Keen, Sam (1986). *Faces of the enemy: Reflections of the hostile imagination.* San Francisco: Harper & Row.

Kennedy, Daniel, & Kerber, August (1973). *Resocialization: An American experiment.* New York: Behavioral Publications.

Koenig, Fredrick (1985). *Rumor in the marketplace: The social psychology of commercial hearsay.* Dover, MA: Auburn House.

Kohn, Alfie (1990). *The brighter side of human nature.* New York: Basic Books.

Kollock, Peter, & O'Brien, Jodi (1994). *The production of reality.* Thousand Oaks, CA: Pine Forge.

Kuhn, Manford (1960). Self-attitudes by age, sex, and professional training. *Sociological Quarterly, 1,* 39-55.

Largey, Gale, & Watson, David (1992). The sociology of odors. *American Journal of Sociology, 77,* 1021-1034.

Leinberger, Paul, & Tucker, Bruce (1991). *The new individualists: the generation after the organization man.* New York: HarperCollins.

Levin, Jack (1993). Misery as a turning point for academic success. *Journal of Research in Education, 3,* 3-6.

Levin, Jack, & Arluke, Arnold (1987). *Gossip: The inside scoop.* New York: Plenum.

Levin, Jack, Arluke, Arnold, & Levin, William C. (1992, August). *Powerful elders.* Paper presented at the annual meeting of the American Sociological Association.

Levin, Jack, & Fox, James A. (1991). *Mass murder: America's growing menace.* New York: Berkley.

Levin, Jack, & Levin, William C. (1980). *Ageism: Prejudice and discrimination against the elderly.* Belmont, CA: Wadsorth.

Levin, Jack, & Levin, William C. (1982). *The functions of discrimination and prejudice* (2nd ed.). New York: Harper & Row.

Levin, Jack, & Levin, William C. (1991). Sociology of educational late-blooming. *Sociological Forum, 6,* 661-680.

Levin, Jack, & McDevitt, Jack (1993). *Hate crimes: The rising tide of bigotry and bloodshed.* New York: Plenum.

Levin, William C. (1988). Age stereotyping: College student evaluations. *Research on Aging, 10,* 134-148.

Leyton, Elliot (1986). *Compulsive killers.* New York: Washington News.

Lowenthal, Leo (1961). *Literature, popular culture and society.* New York: Prentice Hall.

Lurie, Alison (1981). *The language of clothing.* New York: Random House.

Lynd, Robert S., & Lynd, Helen M. (1929). *Middletown: A study in American culture.* New York: Harcourt Brace.

Marx, Karl, & Engels, Frederick (1964). *On religion.* New York: Schocken.

Mead, George Herbert (1934). *Mind, self and society.* Chicago: University of Chicago Press.

Mecca, Andrew, Smelser, Neil, & Vasconcellos, John (Eds.). (1989). *The social importance of self-esteem.* Berkeley: University of California Press.

Merry, Sally E. (1984). Rethinking gossip and scandal. In Donald Black (Ed.), *Toward a general theory of social control.* Orlando, FL: Academic Press.

Merton, Robert K. (1957). *Social theory and social structure.* Glencoe, IL: Free Press.

Milgram, Stanley (1974). *Obedience to authority: An experimental view*. New York: Harper & Row.

Millman, Marcia (1980). *Such a pretty face*. New York: Simon & Schuster.

Mirowsky, John, & Ross, Catherine (1989). *Social causes of psychological distress*. New York: Aldine de Gruyter.

Newman, Katherine (1988). *Falling from grace: The experience of downward mobility in the American middle class*. New York: Free Press.

Ogburn, William F. (1950). *Social change*. New York: Viking. (Original work published 1922)

Oliner, Samuel, & Oliner, Pearl (1988). *The altruistic personality*. New York: Free Press.

Orbach, Susie (1978). *Fat is a feminist issue*. New York: Paddington.

Phillips, David (1983). The impact of mass media violence on U.S. homicides. *American Sociological Review, 48*, 560-568.

Phillips, Kevin (1990). *The politics of the rich and the poor*. New York: Random House.

Portes, Alejandro, & Rumbaut, Ruben G. (1990). *Immigrant Americans: A portrait*. Berkeley: University of California Press.

Reiman, Jeffrey (1989). *The rich get richer and the poor get prison* (3rd ed.). New York: John Wiley.

Riesman, David et al. (1950). *The lonely crowd*. New Haven, CT: Yale University Press.

Ritzer, George (1993). *The McDonaldization of society*. Newbury Park, CA: Pine Forge.

Ritzer, George (1995). *Expressing America*. Thousand Oaks, CA: Pine Forge.

Rose, Arnold (1962). Reactions against the mass society. *Sociological Quarterly, 3*, 310-319.

Rosenhan, David (1973). On being sane in insane places. *Science, 179*, 250-258.

Rosenthal, Robert, & Jacobson, Lenore (1968). *Pygmalion in the class-room*. New York: Holt.

Rosnow, Ralph, & Fine, Gary (1976). *Rumor and gossip: The social psychology of hearsay*. New York: Elsevier.

Sampson, Robert, & Laub, John (1994). *Crime in the making: Pathways and turning points through life*. Cambridge, MA: Harvard University Press.

Shibutani, Tamotsu (1966). *Improvised news*. Indianapolis: Bobbs-Merrill.

Sieber, Samuel (1981). *Fatal remedies*. New York: Plenum.

Sipes, Richard G. (1973). War, sports, and aggression. *American Anthropologist, 75*, 64-86.

Tumin, Melvin (1953). Some principles of stratification: A critical analysis. *American Sociological Review, 18*, 387-394.

Weber, Max (1958). *The Protestant ethic and the spirit of capitalism*. New York: Scribner's.

Whyte, William H. (1956). *The organization man*. New York: Simon & Schuster.

Wilson, William J. (1987). *The truly disadvantaged*. Chicago: University of Chicago Press.

Wright, Charles, R. (1986). *Mass communication: A sociological perspective*. New York: Random House.

Zimbardo, Philip C., Haney, Craig, & Banks, William C. (1973, April 8). A Pirandellian prison. *New York Times Magazine*.

Zurubavel, Eviatar (1981). *Hidden rhythms: Schedules and calendars in social life*. Chicago: University of Chicago Press.

Index

Italy, xenophobia in, 146

J

Jackson, Jesse, 65
Jacobson, Lenore, 69
Jaffe, Rona, 84, 86
Jenson, Arthur, 149
Jewishness, as a stereotype, 55
"Jogger, Central Park," 36
Johnson, Richard, 177
Jones, Landon Y., 45
Journalism Quarterly, 174

K

Kalberg, Stephen, 107
Kanter, Rosabeth M., 90
Kantrowitz, Barbara, 185-186
Katz, Jack, 130
Kaufman, Debra Renee, 17
Kazarosian, Marsha, 98, 99
Keen, Sam, 45
Kennedy, Daniel, 70
Kerber, August, 70
Killer, serial, 37, 113, 125
Kinsey, Alfred, 171
Koenig, Fredrick, 167, 178
Kohn, Alfie, 46
Kollock, Peter, 70
Kuhn, Manford, 72

L

Lamm, Richard, 144
Language of Clothing, The (Lurie),
    177
Largey, Gale, 45
Las Vegas Sun, 175
Laub, John, 71
Law school, socialization in, 71, 72
Leal, David, 40
"Legal Education as Corporate
    Ideology" (Granfield), 71
Leinberger, Paul, 87-89, 90
Lesbians. *See* Homosexuals
Levine, Robert, 16

Levin, Jack, 17, 45, 83, 108, 114,
    127, 130, 151, 178
Levin, William C., 10, 13, 17, 108,
    143
Leyton, Elliott, 130
Libel, lawsuit on, 175
Life chances, 137-138
Lifestyle, alternative, 95-96
Lonely Crowd, The, 107
Lorenz, Konrad, 38-39
Los Angeles Times, 152
Lowenthal, Leo, 26
Lurie, Alison, 177
Lynd, Helen, 171
Lynd, Robert, 171

M

McDevitt, Jack, 45
McDonaldization of Society, The
    (Ritzer), 90, 107
Madsen, Richard, 46, 184
Mall, shopping, rumor about,
    168-170
Management, philosophy, 89
Manson, Charles, 123, 124
Marx, Karl, 25, 157, 158, 177
Mass Murder (Levin and Fox), 127,
    130
Max Weber (Gerth and Mills), 130
"Max Weber's Types of
    Rationality" (Kalberg), 107
Mead, George Herbert, 69
Mecca, Andrew, 69
*Media, Audience, and Social
    Structure* (Ball-Rokeach and
    Cantor), 70
Medical school, socialization in,
    71, 72
Menshu, Rigoberta, 40
Mental illness:
    and socialization, 120-121
    study on feigned, 121
    See also Deinstitutionalization
Men and Women of the Corporation
    (Kanter), 90
Merry, Sally E., 178